Embower

WEALTH

I AM

TARA JACKSON

Thank you for all your support! Much love, Tara ♡

ISBN:
978-1-913590-65-9 (Paperback)
978-1-913590-66-6 (ebook)

Cover design by Lynda Mangoro.
Author photograph by Brendan Jackson.

The Unbound Press
www.theunboundpress.com

Hey unbound one!

Welcome to this magical book brought to you by The Unbound Press.

At The Unbound Press, we believe that when women write freely from the fullest expression of who they are, it can't help but activate a feeling of deep connection and transformation in others. When we come together, we become more and we're changing the world, one book at a time!

This book has been carefully crafted by both the author and publisher with the intention of inspiring you to move ever more deeply into who you truly are.

We hope that this book helps you to connect with your Unbound Self and that you feel called to pass it on to others who want to live a more fully expressed life.

With much love,

Nicola Humber

Founder of The Unbound Press
www.theunboundpress.com

KIND WORDS ABOUT EMBODIED WEALTH

Embodied Wealth is completely different from any other book I've read about wealth or abundance (and I've read a LOT of them over the years!) In this magical book Tara manages to capture the essence of wealth and how we can embody more of this in the world. There's no striving here – the journey Tara takes us on in these pages is gentle, yet potently transformational. As I read Embodied Wealth, I could feel myself opening to more of ME and through that process a more expansive experience of wealth. You can't help but be impacted in the most powerful way by this beautiful book!
Nicola Humber, Transformational Writing Mentor

Embodied Wealth landed graciously with me at a time when, although I didn't consciously know it until I began reading, I had been awaiting its vast and all-encompassing wisdom for a long time. Tara's work is always beyond inspirational and thought-provoking and this book is no exception. Changing the collective idea of wealth has never been more needed and more pertinent than it is right now; as Tara invites us to see, wealth is so much more than money and material possessions. The teachings shared in this book are in themselves part of the new, more expansive perception of wealth that Embodied Wealth has opened up in me. The book gifts the reader an invitation to explore, to go deeper into the infinite possibility and magic of being all that we can be, because now is the time to break old moulds. Thank you, Tara, for birthing this truly amazing work. Already I can't wait to dive into it again!
Em Mulholland, Shamanic Practitioner and Word Doula

Embodied Wealth is a journey and guide into fully realising yourself. Tara's words are a balm to any weary soul and traveller who has found themselves lost yet still trudging the same path.
This book offers a truly wonderous glimmer of undeniable energy and wisdom. So many insights, nudging guidance, bucket loads of encouragement. Each page and chapter weaves poetry and practicality. How else can you embody without this?
Embodied Wealth brings you back home. To Yourself. As you read

the stories and connect with the persuasive and gentle questionings there is a remembering of 'home'. Of All You Have Been. The Divine energy of Feminine Power yet also the Divine Masculine who takes action. In this book, Tara has managed to generously give you her experience of transforming her inner world to creating the wealth in her outer world.

This book is a gift. Truly.

Katherine Louise Jones, Colour Mirrors Teacher and Mentor

You are the wealth you have been longing, seeking and yearning for. This is what Tara enables us to feel and experience in Embodied Wealth. You could open it to any page, and receive an insight or prompt, to reconnect with how and where wealth lives in you. In this way, she makes wealth tangible for us again. Tara also invites us to redefine wealth: to see it as a life where we are living as the truest, most alive versions of ourselves. She reminds us that who we are at our core, is more than enough: it is exactly what we need and what the world needs, now. Embodied Wealth and Embodied Creation are a powerful pair. Used together, these books will support you to step fully into your power and then create what you are being called to create. And their power lies in helping us to remember the way of flow, in harmony with the seasons and the earth. A new way is here, are you ready to begin?

Toni Giselle Stuart, Poet, Performer and Creative Facilitator

Embodied Wealth feels like a breath of fresh air in the arena of abundance and wealth building. This book is nothing like the manifestation claptrap but goes far deeper. It touches upon the very essence of wealth being connected to the innate wisdom of the soul. This book changes the perception of what wealth is and allows the readers to move through a different experience, one that can become a way of life rather than a limited resource to end up with. The nuances of how wealth is perceived, how it intricately weaves into an individual and collective experience of power is beautifully portrayed. It felt like I was taken on a guided journey with the colours of wealth. The spaces of inquiry Tara crafts are perfect for self-reflection and ultimately changing your wealth story because the wealth of one or the deprivation of it affects the all.

Aparna Vemula, Intuitive Coach and Reiki Master

This is a powerful book of activations. I had to read it with a journal in hand because energy would activate while I was reading, and thoughts would come in that unlocked new ways of seeing wealth. Tara's thoughtful writing prompts helped me to ground and integrate her insights. It's a supportive, challenging, optimistic and powerful addition to Tara's collection of "Embodied" books. I feel stronger and clearer in my body after going on this Embodied Wealth journey and I know more layers of insight are waiting for me in future reads of it. Grab your journal, set up sacred space for yourself and let this book reveal more of who you really are.
Jacqui McGinn, Writer, Healer and Japanese and ESOL teacher

Embodied wealth is not just a book, it is a powerful, healing portal that takes you on a journey of reclaiming and rediscovering your true self. Through gentle guidance and loving support it leads you back home, to YOU, to wealth, joy, freedom, and love. It helped me tremendously, and is what I've been looking for on my spiritual path. So simple, yet so profound. Thank you Tara for such a valuable gift!
Tijana Mitrovic, Theta Healer and Intuitive Guide

What if wealth was more than simply an accumulation of material possessions or a steppingstone to power over others? What if wealth was available to more than just the elite few? In this book Tara invites us to open to this possibility. She calls us to turn towards the riches that lie within us and to step into the magic of what happens when we begin to embody "true wealth". Her passion for supporting people to connect with and express their full authentic selves is truly palpable. And her lived experience makes the process all the more approachable. I enjoyed dreaming into the prompts and practices. They helped me uncover not only some unexpected limiting beliefs but also brought more clarity about what I wish to cultivate in my life. Reading this book has left me feeling wealthier and more at home in myself. I am so grateful. Thank you Tara.
Rosalie Kohler, Artist, Writer and Yoga Nidra Facilitator

Embodied Wealth is powerful and potent. The words land ever so softly and ever so profoundly on one's heart. Gentle, thoughtful, probing, challenging, and deeply insightful; Tara ushers us into a deeper, more whole experience of abundance. Embodied Wealth

is poetry and guidance intertwined together, inviting the reader to themselves and embodied wealth.
Char Newswanger, Branding Consultant

I felt so many synchronicities when I started reading. From the journey back to oneself prompted by Covid to not feeling wealthy. This beautiful jewel of a book is for anyone wishing to go to the next level in their soul work. Tara takes the reader by the hand and dances you into luscious and nourishing places you had forgotten.
Sarah Lloyd, PR Alchemist and Author

Embodied Wealth is a must-read for those who are looking for inspiration for their own self-development journey. It is full of honest shares and deep insights. Tara holds nothing back, instead she opens her heart to share her steps to heal and let go of old patterns, limiting beliefs and even stuff from past lives. It is authentic as well as magical. You are always invited to take action, too, due to many prompts or suggestions on how to dive deeper into your own healing journey, for example with the help of colours, so it is also a great and powerful workbook. Tara points out clearly that wealth is so much more than having things, and it can be experienced in many different ways, if you are courageous and bold enough, committed to living your life to the fullest. The content will create a ripple effect of worldwide wealth from within. Thank you so much for this wonderful book.
Sandra von Schmeling, Qigong Teacher, Communicator for Nature, Earth and Tree Wisdom

Embodied Wealth is an inspiring and supportive guide for those seeking a more holistic and expansive experience of discovering their true wealth. Tara successfully weaves her eloquent wisdom, personal stories, spiritual and practical tools together to create a more harmonious and aligned journey. Allow this to challenge your perspectives of what is possible for your life and the wider world.
Elizabeth Gordon, Nature Guide

Embodied Wealth is a deeply personal account of Tara's relationship with wealth and an invitation to go deeper into your own. The question prompts, practices, and included visionings are a helpful guide to illuminate your truth. The section on colour was especially impactful. Embodied Wealth is highly relevant for all stages of life; I see myself returning to these pages time and time again.

Angel Ludwig, Founder of Gait a Conscious Organisational Design Firm

This is a very refreshing and much needed book, the honesty and transparency is admirable. The prompts sent me diving deep within, emerging with new found wisdom and wealth and I can see this being a 'go-to' book for many a decade.

Meron Shapland, Energy Medicine and 'SoulScape Your Life' Therapist

This is much needed narrative about money, wealth, and abundance in this day and age. With so many buzzwords and ideologies centred around "manifestation", "dream home", "dream job", and the rampant materialism in modern society Tara investigates what wealth actually means, how we can make peace with our relationship with money, and do so in a way that is of benefit to us all.

Embodied Wealth does more than provide information; Tara holds you in her loving-kindness that can be felt in every page. She acknowledges everyone from all walks of life and encourages the reader to intuitively approach the book – no rush or pressure or need to read it cover-to-cover and try to "fix" yourself. When I come across the rare book that brings me peace and understanding— rather than feeling like I need to know more, do more, be more – I keep it close to me.

Instead of overwhelming you with information, it asks you to tap into what's already there. It helps you to feel, understand, and release. If you're a right-brained kind of person who loves to study but have your best insights when you're not even trying – this is for you. If you're an empath, this is for you. If you're a lightworker, this is for you. If you're feeling called to the Age of Aquarius, this is for you. If you don't identify with any of this but want to relieve stress, anxiety, and depression from the inside – this is for you. If you're looking to truly love yourself and not treat yourself as someone who's a perpetual project to be fixed anymore —this is for you.

Laura Nadia, "The Vegan Dharma Coach", Intuitive Guide, Mindfulness and Embodiment Coach, Podcast Host

I read a lot of personal development books, and I can say, hand on heart, this is one of my new favourites. I couldn't put it down, and I want to buy copies for all of my friends. Embodied Wealth is full of love, lessons, and beauty, giving the reader a new perspective on what it means to truly be wealthy in mind, body, and spirit. Tara's approach to wealth is refreshing and so very needed in today's modern life. Written in easy-to-understand language yet full of deep wisdom, this fantastic book is a must-read for anyone who wants to reframe their approach to wealth and live a more abundant, fulfilling life!

Jesse Lynn Smart, Writing and Editing Services

Embodied Wealth is a gift that the world parched of embodied, aligned, infused abundance so needs at this time. The perfect medicine, these gentle vignettes, invitations to self-enquiry, and creative quests offer a beautifully paced yet potent portal to radical change.

Tara's incredible source-infused writing continues to weave it's kaleidoscope of rich colours within our souls, our cells, and our human experience. Dive in, immerse yourself, and be amazed by what unfolds.

Jo Gifford, Author, Writer, Co-creation Side-kick for Magic Sparking Change Makers

For my youngest brother Sean.
Words can't even begin to express what a gift you are. Getting 'stuck'
with you at the beginning of Covid was one of the best things that has
ever happened for me. You brought me back to myself, you grounded
me, you mirrored me and made me face the parts of myself that
needed holding. You made me feel like I have a family again, like I
belong. You reminded me what truly matters – presence, love, joy and
laughter. I love you.

CONTENTS

Section 4: Claiming Your I AM

WELCOME

Hello, my fellow human,

Welcome! I am truly honoured that you have decided to pick up Embodied Wealth and hope that its energy and words add something to your life.

This book shares some of my journey and things that have supported me along the way to truly becoming more and more of myself, as this is what I deeply believe true wealth is. To claiming my power as a creative soul. To owning my gifts and talents. To holding, healing, acknowledging and integrating all parts of myself. To being me, and stepping into my I AM.

At the time of writing, I feel like I am coming to the end (or natural plateau – as is it ever really the end?) of an intense 13-year journey of growth and transformation, with a particularly accelerated deep dive in the last two and a half years where I initially got 'stuck' back in my childhood home in Kenya due to Covid. I have been immersed in multiple modalities – healing, coaching, programmes, courses, books, journeying, art, you name it – to heal, to find my way, and to come back home to myself.

Through all this 'work', what I have discovered is that it is a peeling back of all the layers, beliefs, patterns, stories, conditioning and more that I have taken on. It's holding the trauma and un-met needs my body carries. Giving myself more love than I ever received, but needed. It's honouring all of me and championing myself in the way that I would someone I deeply love. It's trusting in the journey and leaning into the support available from the physical and non-physical. It's taking the steps (however small they may be), showing up for myself, to truly be all I am here to be.

As I have done this, I find that I am able to step into a life that I create. A life that feels good. A life that I love. And as I let go of all the expectations and parts that aren't truly me, I align more and more with my truth and am able to give back, and be so much more for others and this planet.

My hope is for you to do the same too. For you to be all that YOU truly are.

All my love,
Tara

⑉IVING IN

A little side note before I share more on 'diving in': this book is actually the 'twin' (it came four months later) to my book *Embodied Creation*, which is all about consciously co-creating for the good of the whole. As I was writing *Embodied Creation*, I realised that I was actually feeling the energy of, and trying to write, two books. Then having let go of some of it for the final book, it made it very clear there was still another book that wanted to be written, knocking loudly on my metaphorical door less than a week after *Embodied Creation* officially was released, which is this one – *Embodied Wealth.*

They link very closely to one another, as I truly believe that we are all here to create, and as we create, we tune into our limitless potential, embodying more of our power and our I AM. It's the systems and structures we are born into, the conditioning, beliefs, and stories we carry and tell ourselves that hold so many of us back.

One of these 'beliefs' that stood out for me throughout writing this book is that I have a tendency to over-complicate things. I often feel that if it's not hard work or if it's too easy, then something must be wrong. This was mirrored in what came through in the words – it's a collection of short pieces, each one very simple. Also writing it was ... easy! I was often guided by the soul of the book to take space and 'Chill the fuck out' (the book's actual words), and would freak out as I knew I had such a limited timeframe to write in (it wanted to come out into the world in less than four months from idea to final book). But, when I honoured this, it flowed, and it was such a beautiful confirmation of the ease and simplicity that we can all tune into. Also, in my opinion, a powerful metaphor for creating wealth in our lives.

Embodied Wealth is split up into a few parts.

1. **What is wealth?** – This section shares some of my reflections on wealth, what it means in our current (particularly Western) society, and it invites you to deepen or perhaps even redefine your relationship with it so you can truly embody it on all levels.

2. **Letting go** – This part talks about some of the things that can come up that might be holding you back or stopping you from fully claiming your I AM, from stepping into your magnificence and greatness. This section is by no means exhaustive and is, at the end of the day, based on *my* experience (and from people I know). There might be things coming up for you that aren't included, and so I always encourage you to acknowledge where you are at and what is rising for you.

3. **Holding and support** – This section includes some ways to support yourself to move through anything that might be rising that's holding you back, or stopping you from fully claiming your authentic power and embodying wealth. As mentioned above, if the specific support you need isn't here, do find the resources and help that are relevant to you. You can also ask for help or guidance from someone you trust, or from the unseen (there is so much available to us here), and know that it will come to you.

4. **Claiming your I AM** – This final section is a deeper invitation to step into and own your full self. It includes '**The colours of wealth**', which share a number of messages, guidance, stories and inspiration to support you, based on the psychology of colour and how it is a mirror for what is going on inside of us on a conscious and unconscious level. It invites you to be more intuitive in your approach and trust what colour or colours you are drawn to or repelled by to receive what you need right now.

There is no right or wrong way to 'use' this book. Maybe you want to read it cover to cover and take what resonates and leave what doesn't. Perhaps you want to use the whole book like an oracle deck and pick a page at random, or scan through the contents page, seeing what you are drawn to, trusting it will give you what you need. You could pick a section that you feel called to and work with it, then move on to another. You may decide to focus on 'The colours of wealth' and their individual colour messages as you feel into what you need right now.

Whatever you decide, the only thing I recommend is keeping it simple. As I shared above, this is something that has truly been emphasised to me throughout the writing of this book, so I want to pass on that message.

Keep. It. Simple.

At the end, there is a short closing with some final thoughts from me, as well as a few further resources, including ways to connect with me, if you want to go deeper.

Happy diving in!

A LITTLE OF MY JOURNEY

When I first got back to Kenya after almost 20 years of living in London (where in a nutshell, I had attended university, worked in many jobs and also started my own business), right before the pandemic took over the world, I wasn't feeling very wealthy. I had done a lot of healing and work on myself and was starting to come to a place where I actually liked myself (I spent years feeling low and unhappy with myself, which I share more about in my book *Embodied*), but so much in my life felt chaotic and uncertain.

I was leaving a relationship and home that had held me, friends and nearby family, and all that I had known for my entire adult life, to come back to my family home where I had grown up, but also felt quite disconnected from. My worldly possessions were all in a small storage locker in the south of England, where I planned to move to when I returned to the UK a couple of months later.

I was in that space in between, that time when you have left one thing and what is next isn't quite known yet.

It felt uncomfortable.

It felt scary.

It felt overwhelming and confusing as I juggled thoughts of feeling like a failure for not being able to make it work (whatever that meant to me at the time) in London and having to return back to my parents in my late 30s, with wondering what was next and if I could truly make it work with my own business. I had also just let my first business in health coaching go, and the idea for my current one, Empathpreneurs® (working to support empaths in business), was still just that – an idea.

We all know what happened next. My plans to return to the UK went out of the window when the world went into lockdown just one month after I arrived in Kenya. I was stuck in a place I didn't want to be, my parents got stuck in France where they had been

– intending to stay for only a few weeks – and I was left alone with my brother, Sean, with multiple special needs (we did have his wonderful carers too).

I was thrown back into my childhood life, albeit as an adult now, but it's amazing what being in your childhood home will do for your memories and forcing you to face what's been shoved down for years. I think like many (and I fully acknowledge my privilege here), Covid gave me an opportunity to really look at, feel, and experience what I thought I had left behind. I had no choice but to go into all the feelings, emotions, fears, feelings, and everything that was rising as I seemed to live out experiences from my childhood once again that were triggered by the myriad of things rising from being back in this situation.

Why do I tell you this? To illustrate how much of an inner journey it is to experiencing true wealth, and it's something I had to live, breathe, and deeply embody to feel as wealthy as I do today – in all senses of the word. I was being called to dive deep into my shadows to face what needed holding, healing, and often releasing, to help myself truly align with all I am here to be – my truth, my essence, my wholeness.

Many of the experiences and triggers that rose for me went into my core wounds around feeling un-wanted, not belonging, feeling rejected and abandoned, and as a result of that, un-worthy and un-lovable. All things that stopped me from truly being me. Some of these you might relate to as they are very common threads woven amongst us.

As these feelings surfaced and old stories, memories, and beliefs bubbled up, I chose to hold them, re-parent myself, let them go, ask for guidance and support if I found myself coming up against something that I couldn't find a way around or through (I also had some powerful one-to-one coaching), and above all, find a new, more empowering story to take forward with me.

The tools that supported me most with this are what I mostly use with clients – deep visualisations and journeys, energy work, lots of journaling (and doing a lot of belief re-writing), and colour psychology.

The colour psychology system I was introduced to by a friend and subsequently trained in is Colour Mirrors. It is a set of bottles with oil and water in (which you can bathe in, rub on your body, look at, or whatever you are called to do – for example, I painted how some of them made me feel), each in different colours and colour combinations. Each one shows how what we are drawn to and/or repelled by can shed light on where there might be something inside that needs to be healed.

Each colour is a mirror to what is going on inside on a conscious and subconscious level, and as you dive into the meaning of each colour, it can powerfully (sometimes gently, sometimes more intensely) help you face what needs to come up. Above all, it supports your body to release and integrate the experience, as colour has such a visceral effect on the body. Each colour can also suggest a possible past life where there might be something in your energy field you are still holding on to, and as you are drawn to certain colours, you might be taken on a journey to that time and place, or be shown something else to support your healing or for you to truly 'get' something in your body – I certainly was!

This is what I share with you in the 'Colours of wealth' section at the end. Each colour bottle that I worked with gave me a different message, story, or some form of guidance, which deeply impacted me, even if only in a subtle way, so my intention is to share these experiences in various ways to support you.

SECTION 1: WHAT IS WEALTH?

In this section, I share some ways to look at wealth that go beyond what it currently is defined as, including how it links to power, and truly stepping into and claiming your authentic power – your I AM – as your truth. I share some ways that you might start to deepen or perhaps re-define your own relationship with it.

ʄNCIENT WEALTH

There's an ancient thread of wealth that weaves its way like a current amidst us all.
It's a force of energy that comes from deep within Gaia.
It's alchemical by nature.
It's powerful, magical and wise.

It carries the blueprint and codes of a seed
It aligns with the rhythm of the seasons.
It's here for us to tune into at any time.
It mirrors what we feel inside.

It's here to bring in a different way.
A way that creates from the inside out.
A way that embodies all that we desire to feel, be and experience.
A way that knows we can all be wealthy.

MONEY

I start here as this is where the majority are at with what they feel wealth is. It's what I certainly believed for many years, and my journey in pursuit of more money, as well as my ongoing relationship with it, has certainly been one of the greatest catalysts for more self-awareness, self-discovery, self-growth and, at the end of the day, helping me to become more me, and what I today define wealth as.

I grew up in one of, if not 'the', richest suburbs of Nairobi, Kenya. I went on a private school bus to school, where I received a private international education, had friends from all over the world, and got to travel to see family and friends in the US, Canada, and Europe every summer. I grew up privileged.

Literally next to the leafy suburb that is the bubble our house was in, there is a huge slum. We had people working for us, who are like family, who live in much, much less-off situations. There is a significant divide and contrast between the wealthy and the poor in Nairobi. When I left the cocoon of that environment for university in London, I realised how marked that divide really was, as perspective is everything. But I'll come back to that in a moment.

Growing up, I also vividly remember a couple of family members and friends of my parents who lived a 'regular' life back in the UK telling my sister, brother and me how spoilt we were and that we had silver spoons in our mouths growing up.

As a child and sensitive person, this was incredibly hurtful and confusing for me as it was just the life I was brought into. All my friends in school were the same, and I thought I was a generally good, kind, and caring person – so why was I being judged based on something out of my control? Deep down, I hated the contrasts between the life I got to live compared with the majority of local Kenyans. I always felt the unfairness of it, but I shoved these feelings down, swept along by life happening 'to' you, as it tends to do when you are in your childhood and teens. Also, I didn't know what I could do about it back then, except be kind and generous to others, which I always was.

Back to when I left Kenya, starting a completely new life in a new city. Here, I was just a 'regular' person. Of course, there are people living in both wealth and poverty in London, but it felt different here. I wasn't on one end of the spectrum, I was somewhere in the middle, and that felt safer. It felt like I belonged more.

But just as that was settling in and I felt like I was going through the same things as other friends – stuff like too much month for my money, and having to eat things like dried packet noodles to save money – I received a trust fund that had been left to me by my mum, who had passed away when I was eight. Again, this put me in a different situation; it brought back all the contrasts I'd felt having money when others didn't, and this time it was worse as I decided it was money I was receiving instead of having a mum, so I didn't want any of it.

I began to give it all away and use it left, right, and centre.

It seemed to be the catalyst for many thoughts and feelings that had been bubbling under the surface – from the sadness I felt about the unfairness of the world, to seeing so much struggle to even survive and get by – and I began to create a new narrative for myself that went something along these lines.

'Why do I have more than others? Who am I to have money? Who am I to have things come to me so easily? I hate that I am privileged. Surely if I have less, there will be more for others. If I am struggling, maybe people will like me more for me and not see me as some spoilt, rich kid.'

Even if you haven't been brought up in the same way, you may relate to this, as it's not an uncommon story.

This began a long journey of trying to have less than, to be less than, so I stopped standing out (even though I probably felt like I stood out more than I actually did). I started to spend everything I had on treating others. Or on food, alcohol, and clothes (as if you've read my first book, *Embodied*, you'll know I also experienced a number of addictions in my late teens and twenties). I was always generous with money, but I took it to a new level. That money soon finished, and I began to take out loans, credit cards, and overdrafts to keep up, and I still continued to pay for everyone. I ended up thousands of pounds in debt.

Since that first time, I have yo-yo'd back and forth between it all: I've had money, I've gone back into debt, I've had money again, I've gone back into debt.

It was only when I really began to dive into my money story and beliefs around privilege and my upbringing, healing, holding, and releasing what I've needed to that I felt a powerful shift. I have been able to tell myself and believe that my being in a situation of having less than or suffering helps nobody, and it certainly doesn't help me. By allowing myself to own who I am, and stepping into my privileged position, I can embody my strengths that I deeply believe we need at this time (we are all needed to bring forward our strengths – no matter what they are). I can bring care and compassion to others and help in the many ways I have always wanted to. I can hold space without judgement, which is sometimes the most powerful thing, as we all need to be heard, witnessed, and seen for who we are. I can support others in less privileged situations, empower people, and I can be a vessel, a faucet if you will, for abundance (including prosperity) to flow through to reach others.

I am only fully stepping into this (and I still have times where my stories and beliefs around privilege pop up to be held and re-written, as they run deep), and every day/week/month I try to do more, give more, help others more, but this time from a fully empowered place of choice, not because I am trying to avoid something, or feeling obligated in any way. I am also very open to new ways of doing this. Ways that benefit on multiple levels and, above all, begin to empower others, so that the change has a ripple effect that begins to affect change on a larger scale, rather than something that is a one- or few-times-off.

Privilege is power in our society. But, the way I see it is that you, we, those of us holding it in any way, have a responsibility to use it in a way to benefit the whole and, in particular, those less privileged in any way, rather than deny it, or use it only for ourselves, or for power over another or others. Privilege in the case of having money means that survival isn't something that you have to think about every single day. Instead, you can use that energy in ways that support others, or perhaps to learn more about how you can do this. It can also be caring for yourself deeply and in a way that is embodied so that you can show up more for others.

Money is, of course, also absolutely integral to wealth, at least in today's current economic system, as it is the tool of exchange that allows us to experience more and help create lives that bring more of the feelings we want to feel. It allows us to meet our basic needs – including having food, shelter, and security. It buys experiences such as travel, learning, and trying new things. It can also be an incredible mirror to what is going on inside of you as, if you look at your relationship with money, it can bring up fears, beliefs, stories, and anything else that might be coming up, stopping you from living a life you truly desire.

EMBODIED WEALTH PROMPTS

- *What's your relationship with money like right now?*
- *How would you like it to be?*

DISMANTLING WEALTH

When I first began writing this book, I decided to look up the actual meaning of the word 'wealth'. It is basically described as an abundance of valuable possessions or money, or plenty of something that is desirable.

The first thing I thought is that this doesn't fully resonate with me, the journey I've been on, and where I am today. I get that wealth is those things, but that feels very old-paradigm, and scarcity driven. To me, wealth is so much more!

I feel that wealth is a state of being. It comes from the inside and is a way of feeling, living, and creating your life. It can be applied to any area of your life, such as your finances, relationships, home, health, etc., but at the end of the day is something quite unique to each of us and fundamentally comes down to our individual values.

For example, my top values/feelings that I want to experience in my life are freedom, love, connection, beauty, peace, and joy. How I go about experiencing these things in my life will completely differ from someone else who perhaps has similar values. How I apply those values to different areas of my life will change as I grow and evolve, but ultimately they form the basis for creating a wealthy life, as I seek to experience them. As I begin to feel these different things in different areas of my life, I am embodying wealth.

When we look at wealth from this perspective – a way of life, rather than something we have to accumulate – it is something that we can all have. It is something that brings deep meaning and purpose to our lives. It's not about competing or fighting for the most resources and trying to hoard all the wealth. It is something that creates a new world, one that honours our differences and similarities. One that honours this planet.

We stop ourselves from experiencing wealth due to the systems and cultures we have been brought up in. We have a way to go absolutely to truly embody wealth in this new way and to shift from seeing it as something to be accumulated, to seeing it as a lived experience that is cultivated from the inside out, but this change is happening. If you are here reading this, you are likely one of those people here to be a part of this change.

As I sat further with the word 'wealth' – letting myself feel it, what it means, playing with it, inviting it to guide me – it deeply felt to me that wealth is being the most you that you can possibly be. It's owning who you are – your greatness, your magnificence. It's not playing small, dimming to fit in. It's letting go of stories, limitations and lack. It's knowing that you are more powerful than you have ever been told or been allowed to be, and there might be a little spark deep, deep inside of you that knows this to be true. AND, above all, it's letting yourself step into this and actually BE all that you are. It's embodying YOU.

WEALTH IS UNLIMITED

If wealth is a lived experience and something we can cultivate from within, the potential is unlimited. It can be anything and everything, and we are much closer to embodying it than many of us might think.

That's the vision I saw of this book's essence when I first connected to it (if you are new to connecting to the essence of your creations to co-create with them, you can find out more about it, including how to do it, in my book *Embodied Creation*) – which was a tree, deeply rooted, with branches of wealth reaching into all corners of the globe. Each branch was carrying a different quality, energy, and feeling that we can experience, such as joy, love, connection, peace, love, etc. It was vibrant, colourful, and abundantly overflowing with limitless wealth. It was something we can all feel, even if only for a moment, no matter our circumstances or situation.

And as we experience wealth as a feeling in our bodies, on an energetic level, we also can begin to physically manifest more of it into our lives as we become a vibrational match to it.

Activating Wealth in Your Life

To begin to activate wealth in your life, I invite you to feel into what wealth means to you. A way to do this is to begin to vision into and choose what you would like to experience in your life.

So many of us have no idea when it comes to what we would like, as we are so used to living the lives we are told to, within the conditioning and beliefs we have been brought up with and picked up from people in our lives, as well as the system that currently presides. Of course, things are changing, and there are many people that don't fall into this category of not knowing, but I feel it safe to say that the majority still do.

Here are a few prompts to start to feel into this and activate and create wealth in your life.

Embodied Wealth Prompts

- *What does wealth mean to you right now?*
- *What values/feelings are important to you right now to experience in your life? There is a list below with a few examples to help you get started, which you can also add to (and this can, of course, change at any time).*
- *How would you like to feel in the different areas in your life? E.g. home, relationships, health, finances, career, family, free time, personal growth, spirituality, etc. (feel free to add any that you like).*
- *What one action step could you take to begin to feel the way you desire in a certain area in your life? For example, if you would like to feel more nurtured in your relationships, you could do something that nurtures your relationship with yourself, like cooking a delicious meal, spending time in nature, taking a soothing bath, or simply being with yourself and tuning into your body and asking it what it needs.*

Abundant
Adventurous
Aligned
Awe-inspiring
Beautiful
Bold
Brave
Calm
Childlike
Committed
Compassionate
Confident
Connected
Conscious
Consistent
Cosy
Courageous
Creative
Deep
Delicate
Delicious
Dependable
Devoted
Efficient
Embodied
Empathic
Empowered
Energised
Explorative
Expansive
Fearless
Feminine
Flowing

Free
Fun
Gentle
Grateful
Grounded
Happy
Harmonious
Healthy
Heart-opening
Held
Hopeful
Individual
Inspiring
Intelligent
Intuitive
Joyful
Juicy
Kind
Leadership
Light
Limitless
Loving
Luminous
Luscious
Magical
Masculine
Mastery
Mysterious
Open
Optimistic
Over-flowing
Passionate
Peaceful

Playful
Powerful
Precious
Present
Productive
Prosperous
Purposeful
Rich
Safe
Secure
Sensitive
Sensual
Serene
Shining
Soft
Soulful
Sparkling
Spiritual
Spontaneous
Stable
Strong
Successful
Supportive
Thoughtful
Tranquil
Trusting
Unbound
Unique
Warm
Wealthy
Wise
Wonder-full

SEEING WEALTH DIFFERENTLY

I invite you to tune into the energy of wealth so that you can begin to see, feel, hear, and know it in a new way. Read through the visualisation words first, which explain a way that you can do this.

Visualisation

I invite you to close your eyes or lower your gaze and begin to breathe into your lower belly. Slowing your breath down, deeply breathing into your body.

Feel where your body touches the ground. Feel the air on your skin. Spend a few moments here, drawing your energy inside, away from the outside world.

Now, invite the energy of wealth to come to you in whatever way it wants to. It may be a spark of energy, a colour, a feeling, a knowing. However it appears is always perfect, and if nothing does, that's also fine.

Spend a few moments simply allowing the energy of wealth to be with you, breathing into it, letting it guide you.

Then, from this more inward space of connection, I invite you to answer whichever of these prompts you feel drawn to.

- Wealth feels like...
- Wealth wants me to know right now...
- If wealth was a plant/flower/tree, it would be...
- The unexpected/lesser-known thing about wealth is...
- If wealth was a colour, it would be...
- I can embody my wealth by...

I AM WEALTH

I invite you to write down or speak the words, 'I am wealth' three times or more if you choose. Then begin to feel into your body and see what comes up for you.

This is what came up for me:

I am living as my fullest, free-est self, connected with my limitless potential. I honour my needs deeply. I live in alignment with my body, heart, mind, and soul. I make choices that always feel in integrity and honour myself and others. I look after my body and support it to flourish so that I truly live a thriving physical life. I am deeply excited by life and all the opportunities available to me. I know it won't always be easy, and there may be challenges along the way, but that's okay as I always have me.

These words may serve as an activator, inviting you into the truth of your wealth. Or they may bring up all the reasons you aren't wealth, or something in between. Wherever you are at right now is perfect. If you are more on the side of 'not wealth', how would you like it to feel/be instead? I invite you to begin to tune into that.

WEALTH IS WHO YOU ARE AT YOUR CORE

If asked, 'Who are you?' what is your immediate response?

So often with this question, we reply with what we 'do' in life – what our job is, the work that we do, what we are currently studying. Maybe it's the roles that we have taken on (even if we aren't paid for them), or perhaps it's the social and other identifiers that we have been given, such as our name, nationality, gender, etc.

But I invite you to really feel beneath all that. Who are you at your core?

There might be layers, there might be uncertainty as to who you really are. Often without all the given names and things we do, we don't even know who we are. In our fast-paced and quite-controlled system, we haven't ever been given a chance to feel it. To explore it. To discover it. To get to know it.

Here are a few prompts to begin to feel into this.

- What do you bring just by being you?
- If you had to describe yourself in one word, what would it be?
- If you were to describe yourself when you were a child, what would you say?
- If you were to describe your heart, what would you say?
- If you were to describe your soul, what would you say?
- What excites you?
- What makes your heart happy?
- What brings you joy?
- What brings you pleasure?
- What do you desire to experience?

Your answers to these questions will hopefully begin to give you an idea of who you are beneath all the labels. They will hopefully begin to show you some of the qualities you carry that contribute to your unique essence and spark.

THE WEALTH IN WORDS

For a long time, I have felt that there aren't enough words in the English language to describe some of the feelings, sensations, images, emotions and more that one can feel and experience. They just don't capture the breadth, the expansiveness and sheer vastness of some of the things I have personally felt when I go on visual journeys or the things that my body feels in deep, aligned soul connections with others or even alone.

Perhaps it's my own limited vocabulary. Or maybe the English language needs to evolve.

Much like when I looked up the meaning of the word 'wealth' and found that its literal translation wasn't enough for me, perhaps we need to expand what words mean to us, and not have them mean such fixed and rigid things. A bit like the patriarchy with its systems of control and boxing things in, maybe it's time to feel words – let them live through us, guide us, and feel us too.

This feels like a way to approach wealth.

WEALTHY MOMENTS

I invite you to notice the wealthy moments in your life already, the times which bring you more of the feelings you want to cultivate, and take the time to really appreciate them. Every. Single. Day.

Here are some of mine:

- Giving gifts to others just because.
- A moment of intimacy and connection with someone you love, who loves you back.
- Napping in the afternoon.
- Taking a bath in the middle of the morning.
- Sleeping with no alarm set.
- Deep belly laughs with people you just get and vice-versa.
- Delicious, nourishing food that you can literally feel your body absorbing with glee.
- Popcorn for dinner.
- Appreciating the lushness of nature in its majestic beauty.
- Spending time with my brother, Sean, who is blind, has cerebral palsy and other disabilities, seeing the world from his viewpoint, and deeply appreciating the present moment.
- Getting to work with and support such incredible, beautiful souls from around the globe.
- Creating a business that works on my terms and honours my body's needs.
- Having a healthy body that can run, stretch, move, and feel so alive.
- Deep meditations that take me into other realms, and lucid dreams where I can truly create my reality in the moment.

Plus so much more.

Every single wealthy moment you experience begins to add up over time, and as you feel it deeply in your body, you naturally begin to draw more of it towards you.

WEALTH IN THE CHAKRAS

Much of my work links to the chakras as I find that tapping into these energy centres can be such a powerful way to help us let go of what might be holding us back, as well as actively create harmony and balance holistically in our lives.

Here is how I see each of the chakras infused with the qualities of true wealth. If it resonates, I invite you to feel into each one and see where you are at with it. Do the words feel good to you? What would it take for you to fully align with embodying the qualities of each chakra?

Earth Star
Grounded, deeply rooted and held.

Base/Root
Safe and secure, passionate and alive.

Sacral
In tune with all of my creative potential and power.

Solar plexus
Embodied in my wisdom, my authentic power, and I AM-ness.

Heart
Balanced and harmonious in giving and receiving.

Throat
Fully expressed in all communication.

Third-Eye
Trusting and knowing it is unfolding as it should, and intuitively open to guidance.

Crown
Aligned with your truth, and present to each moment.

Soul Star
Connected to all that is from a place of oneness.

THE POWER IN WEALTH AND THE WEALTH IN POWER

I feel that wealth and power are intertwined in the patriarchal way of living that currently presides and that both have the potential to tune into something more within us than they currently do.

If we look at the traditional meaning of wealth as having an accumulation of things – money, savings, investments, property, etc. – and the definition of power is to have the ability to do something in a certain way, or have influence over others, there is a definite link between the two. Both allude to being in a position of authority by having more than others, plus there is a connection whereby you are able to exchange wealth to feel powerful and assert your power to increase your wealth.

But what if true wealth is stepping into your authentic power, which is your uniqueness, your essence, your you-ness, being able to fully stand in your wholeness and knowing it without question or at the expense of or in comparison with another?

The wealth in authentic power and taking radical responsibility

With authentic power, there is no need to compete or wield it as something for gain or interests which don't satisfy the whole. It instead knows that we are all connected; we all need one another; we need our home – Earth; we need nature and all sentient beings. We are in this together, and by tuning into our individual gifts, we create a world where we are the sum of all our parts and so much more powerful together.

When we are connected to our authentic power, we honour another's qualities and unique essence, we support them to thrive and be all they can be, and we take radical responsibility for how we show up and what we do to seed a world that no longer relies on systems of oppression and control.

Instead of looking outside, blaming and shaming, we start within to begin to heal, release and let go, so that we can embody our true wealth, compassion, kindness, empathy and love. We know that what created the world today is not how a new one will emerge, and we need to look to nature, the ancients, visionaries, and others to bring about this change.

True wealth is a connection to this knowing, this power we each hold within, and above all a commitment to do what it takes to live, breathe, and embody it in each and every way that is calling.

The power of choice

So many of us feel we don't get to choose anything in our lives – we are prisoners of what has been laid out for us, and even if we are liberated from one aspect, we may feel powerless in another.

We are born into systems, societies, and cultures that literally tell us what to do from the moment we no longer scream to be fed. We tell our bodies to eat three meals a day at set times, even if they aren't hungry. We go to school, do homework, and then find a 'proper' job so that we can buy a house, contribute to a pension, and have a family. We get up in the morning, go to work, sleep, and repeat. We save up for a few meagre weeks of holiday every year, and then we have to go back to work, giving the majority of our time to someone else, living for the weekends. We live so out of synch we our natural rhythms and cycles, especially in countries which experience dark winters, as we are *forced* to stick to the same working hours. This then leads to burnout, numerous other health (mental, physical, emotional and spiritual) conditions, and ultimately, a system that is failing the majority.

As we are born into this 'laid out plan', many of us don't realise, or perhaps feel, that we even have a choice. So we often don't even question things or tune into our power (of choice, of our ability to create – which I will go into).

I know this is quite generalised, and many people are not following this path. I also fully acknowledge that privilege plays a part here, as when basic survival is the main priority, it is extremely difficult (but not impossible) to break free from these systems.

But the bottom line is the over-arching conditioning that we feel we don't have a choice in most things, or even if we do, it's still so easy to get stuck or feel trapped in the system in one way or another.

The power to create

Once we start to let go of these systems and ways that don't even allow us time to think, we begin to remember our truth. We begin to remember that we are creative beings, and are actually more powerful than we have likely ever been taught. Wealth is re-claiming your powerful ability to create. It is tuning into the feelings you want to experience, believing in yourself and beginning to create your world from the inside out.

THE POWER IN PERSPECTIVE

Throughout writing *Embodied Wealth*, I found myself in moments of procrastination, not tied to any reason other than when it came down to it, I felt like an imposter. Who was I to write a book on wealth and what I take wealth to mean?

At the time of writing, I am technically homeless with most of my stuff in storage and am living out of a couple of suitcases. Following my inner guidance, I am taking the month off and not launching or inviting in new people to work with me in any way. I am single with no prospects and zero desire to do the whole internet/app dating thing. I have a business that is growing but not where I want it to be yet, and I still have debt I am paying off.

All these things can certainly get to me, and my head can go into overdrive, wondering whether I'll be broke, homeless and alone forever!

Then I have to remind myself it's also all about perspective.

Sure, I would love to have my own home right now, be in a committed and loving relationship, have more stability in my business and life in general, plus some other things.

But... actually, I am totally free right now. I am blessed and privileged to have choices and the health to travel and explore. I have amazing people offering up spare rooms and beds for me. I actually, for the first time in my life, deeply love being with myself. I've always loved quiet time, but now I actively need and want the time to be by myself without filling the space with a TV series or some other distraction. If I was in a relationship, I might not have this luxury of alone time completely on my terms.

I also trust my guidance more and more, as every time I have followed it, things turn out more magical than I could ever imagine. So even though the pause in my business may seem scary and uncertain, it's not the first time, and I deeply trust that there are wonderful things coming – and that in itself is exciting! I also get to enjoy each day and just 'be', which is something I have always wanted to be able to do, and not through the limited holiday days I got in a 'proper job'. I am living the nomadic laptop lifestyle, which again is something I always wanted, even if it's not how I envisioned it all those years ago (when I first began my freelance life in my late 20s).

It's also about seeing the wealth in the little moments and reminding myself of them regularly. I'm definitely learning a lot about embodying wealth and how it's a conscious choice to see and feel it, even when it feels hard – especially when it feels hard.

EMBODIED WEALTH PROMPTS

- *Is there anything in your life right now that doesn't feel good to you that you could perhaps look at in a different, more empowering way?*
- *Where can you see the wealthy moments within it?*

SECTION 2: LETTING GO

This section includes some of the things that can come up on this journey that might be stopping you from fully stepping into your truth. It invites you to feel into them and take what resonates, and leave what doesn't, so that you can let go of what you no longer need.

FEAR

Fear is the number one thing that stops us from embodying wealth. It stops us from stepping into the truth of who we are and what we are capable of.

Fear keeps us in jobs that take all of our energy, relationships that don't serve us, patterns and behaviours that keep us limited and small.

Fear says it's better to always play the safe option, even if it means dulling or limiting yourself, doing something you don't fully want to do.

Fear stops us from taking chances, from stepping out of our comfort zone, from choosing a new experience and an adventure over what we know already.

Fear says it's not safe to put yourself out there. To let yourself shine. To speak up and out. To be the most YOU that you can possibly be.

Of course, we need fear, and if we were faced with a scary situation down a dark alley, our fear would serve us greatly. But many of our fears today (at least in 'modern' society) often come from a younger version of ourself who is still holding on to something (or perhaps from a memory in this lifetime or another, from an experience that may have been something you saw or experienced personally).

EMBODIED WEALTH PROMPTS

- *Where is fear holding you back?*
- *Where is fear stopping you?*
- *Where is fear keeping you safe and small?*

Trust what rises, and I invite you to do one thing today that you normally wouldn't because of fear.

In the next story, I share a bit more about one of my biggest fears, or at least it used to be – snakes – and a different perspective on re-framing this fear.

SNAKES

Growing up in Kenya, I was taught to fear snakes. 'They are evil, the devil incarnate. They are not to be trusted.'

I have a vivid childhood memory of exploring my wild garden alone as a young child, as I loved to do. It was shortly after the rains, and we had this large hole (which seemed big enough to be a swimming pool to me) in one part, which had now become filled with water. There was this snake gliding along the surface of the water, coming towards me. I remember being absolutely mesmerised by it, unable to move as it got closer and closer. The next thing I remember is someone grabbing me out of the way, telling me that it would kill me if I wasn't careful, and rushing me back into safety.

After that, I was petrified of snakes. I couldn't see one, let alone go near one. I would literally feel my stomach turning, palms and soles getting sweaty and the bolt of adrenalin gearing me up to run if there was even the possibility of one being around. Often when we'd go on holiday within Kenya, either camping or by the beach, we'd be much more exposed to the possibility of snakes being around, and I would be on edge lying in bed at night, so afraid that one might come into my mosquito net.

There was this primal fear inside of me that had been switched on.

Over the years, I often wondered why there was this intense fear around snakes (almost everyone I knew also hated and feared snakes), as something about them also mesmerised me.

When I moved to England, far away from the wild snakes as I knew them, I felt safe enough to start looking into them again. My first job after university was working in a PR company, and one of the things I had to do every day was go through the newspapers to check for coverage and stories of interest for our clients. At one particular time, there were a lot of stories about snakes in the news. Anacondas and pythons, to be exact, and they seemed to centre around them eating alligators in Florida, then bursting open as the alligator thrashed around for its life from within! I found myself tentatively looking at the pictures with absolute fascination.

I also heard this story, which might be a complete rumour (I haven't actually ever checked, as it provided something for my curious inner child that I've not ever wanted to dispel), about a pet python that once stopped eating for a few days and began to lie still in its enclosure. Over the course of a few days, perhaps weeks, it started to change shape and size, gradually getting larger, and I was told that this was it preparing its stomach to eat its human 'owner'. That story absolutely enthralled me, and I told it to everyone I knew that would listen.

Without a doubt, there was something about snakes that both kept me hanging on in deep and utter amazement, as well as scared me, but in a nervous, excited way!

I tell you these stories, as when I started connecting to the energy of this book *Embodied Wealth*, (which is how I write my books, and something I explain how to do in my book *Embodied Creation*), I kept on having dreams and visions about snakes. In fact, the first night I felt this book making itself known, I had a dream about an enormous, bright yellow and vivid turquoise cobra dancing in front of me. In another dream, there was a brown python trying to get in the window and speak to me. I have had a baby silver one which was trying to lead me on a journey, but then my alarm went off. I also saw multiple jumping, golden yellow, sparkling ones when this book was coming close to completion.

Snakes have been seen as the enemy and feared throughout time. To give just a few examples (possible spoiler alert) of where this happens, the story of Adam and Eve in The Bible where the snake tempts Eve to eat the forbidden fruit – the apple. In Greek mythology, we have Medusa with her many snake heads, and anyone who stares into her eyes will turn into stone. In *Harry Potter*, Lord Voldemort, the evil nemesis of our protagonist, has a murderous snake companion.

It got me thinking about snakes in general. Why do they both fascinate and incite fear in us? There's something more here that I feel is a mirror to what we hold inside. In many cultures (not all), we have been taught to fear them. They can be absolutely stunning – if you've ever Google imaged them, you'll see just how many magical colours and sizes they come in. They hold such power and magnificence.

As a spirit animal, snake is about transformation and rebirth, as they shed their entire skins (quite a metaphor for letting go on this journey). There is also a deep primal connection of snakes with creation energy – when this energy (also known as Shakti) is felt rising at the base of the spine. It is called 'Kundalini Rising' and can be an integral part of an individual's awakening journey and stepping into their truth.

I feel that they represent something we know is inside of us. Something that we have been taught to be afraid of and not trust! Something that is so innate and connected to our potential. Something that is uniquely us. Something wild and untethered. I feel they connect to the truth of the power and strength that we each hold inside.

This is why you see snakes on the front cover of this book. I want to invite you to go beyond what you have been told/taught and look deeper within.

EMBODIED WEALTH PROMPTS AND PRACTICE

- *How do you feel about snakes?*
- *What could they teach you about your own power and potential?*

I invite you to pick a snake (look online or ask to be shown one through a sign or symbol) and see which one comes to you. Let it be your guide and muse for a while, and see what wants to rise.

FEELING SAFE SO YOU CAN BE FULLY YOU

Feeling safe is one of the most important aspects when it comes to living a life of wealth in every sense of the word.

This, of course, ties into feeling safe on a base survival level – having a roof over your head, food on the table, feeling provided for, not worrying about where the next paycheck is coming from, feeling like you belong and are accepted by others for who you are, to name a few things. When these needs are met and felt on a deep level, a lot can begin to shift, as the fear-based (ancient) part of the brain calms down and the body naturally shifts more into creation and expansion mode.

Sadly, in our current world, this is not true for most. Also, the stress response in many has been so triggered by the current way of living (through fast-paced lives that offer little time for respite, let alone replenishment), that we are often on high alert and in more of a fear-based space. This means that we don't tune into our potentials of creation and expansion. Instead, we constantly worry and stress about our survival, even if things are actually okay in that moment. We hold on tightly under the illusion that we can control our futures, as we feel so unsafe, uncertain and in fear.

Whilst I totally get the uncertainty in the world and acknowledge that some have it easier than others, we can begin to support ourselves where we are at. So that we can begin to tune into creative potentials and ways that have the power to change our reality, and that allow us to be fully ourselves.

EMBODIED WEALTH PRACTICE

I invite you to observe (without judgement or expectation) the feelings that rise in your body, whether they relate to safety or not. The simple act of awareness has the power to literally change the feelings you are experiencing.

WHAT IDENTITIES ARE YOU STILL HOLDING ON TO?

Often times we hold on to identities from our past as they gave us something at the time. Perhaps they provided sanctuary and safety. Maybe they gave a sense of purpose and meaning. They could have helped us to belong. We may have taken them on to dim our light or not stand out too much.

Some of these might include:

- The good one.
- The helpful one.
- The smart one.
- The quiet one.
- The reliable one.
- The broke one.

It's time to let these labels go. It's time to truly step into who you know deep down inside that you are. It's time to let yourself be all you can be. It's time to choose a new way, a new identity that aligns with your magnificence.

EMBODIED WEALTH PROMPTS

- *Just like a snake sheds its skin, I invite you to tune into the truth of who you are inside, what identities are you holding on to that it's time to let go of? What would you like to claim instead?*

THE ENERGY OF LAND AND SPACES

Halfway through writing this book, I moved countries – from one culture to another, one hemisphere to the other, complete contrasts in land, energy, and spaces. From Kenya to London, England.

Now, of course, we pick up on the energy of land and spaces (especially if you are highly sensitive and empathic like I am), and the countries I was moving from and to are both ones I know very well. But, I was completely shocked by what hit me as I re-entered London.

At first, I was boosted by the energy of a change, and excitement about seeing close family and friends that I hadn't seen for over two years. But, as I slowly melted back into the city, I found my energy declining rapidly. I was reminded how easily I pick up on others' energy un-consciously – one minute I felt down, the next angry, the next sad. I felt so un-motivated and wanted to eat carbs to ground, to feel heavy as well as numb me. I wanted to curl up in bed and binge-watch a Netflix show.

I was having to clear my energy and ground almost every hour just to feel like myself! My almost constant flow of inspiration and creative current that I'd been able to access with ease in Kenya was like a trickle of water fast drying up. I didn't feel like me.

I was reminded that this is how I used to feel most of the time without even being consciously aware of it. These past two years in Kenya have certainly opened me up on another level, so I am acutely aware of the energy now. But what I also realised is that this is how so many people live on a daily basis without even being consciously aware of it. This then contributes to our overall feelings and moods, and ability to consciously create more of what we do want in our lives, rather than getting sucked into a vicious cycle of fast-fix mood-elevators such as TV, sugar, or alcohol, or feeling depressed and overwhelmed by it all, powerless to change anything.

I deeply believe that there are places in the world that serve each of us, so whilst London felt too much to me, it is bursting with energy and many people absolutely thrive here. I know for myself to be all I can be, I need to be much more immersed in nature.

EMBODIED WEALTH PROMPT

* *I invite you to feel into the space and area you live and/or work in. Does it inspire and serve you? If not, perhaps you can move or find somewhere to visit regularly that does, to top up.*

1000 DAYS

At the time of writing, I reached a personal milestone of 1000 days alcohol-free.

Since my teens, I've had a rocky relationship with drinking, like many, and my sensitive system felt the effects both long-term and short-term on so many levels – mentally, physically, emotionally, and spiritually (I share some of this journey in my first book *Embodied*).

I was actually being called to let go of drinking for a long time before I eventually did, and would frequently stop for a month or more here and there. When I did, I would start to see glimmers of how I could feel aligned and in flow with my true self. I always came back to it, though, as a lot of my social life living and working in London revolved around drinking, and I also really enjoyed letting loose and connecting with friends in this way. On the other side, there was definitely some self-sabotage going on. But, the signs got louder and louder until they were screaming at me, and I chose to listen and commit to where I was being guided, on a whole new level.

It was on my birthday, two months to the day after *Embodied* came out, that I decided to stop drinking for a year, and that year continued. Reflecting on the almost three years of not drinking, I realise how much alcohol was stopping me from truly stepping into what I am capable of and who I am here to be – from stepping into my wealth.

I would make excuses for everything and would say I wanted one thing but not take the action I was being guided to, to make it happen. I had low-level anxiety and depression on most days, and comfort-ate and escaped in TV shows to numb myself. I had a myriad of health issues that sometimes stopped me from leaving the house. I felt overweight and unattractive, and saying I disliked myself would be putting it mildly. My self-esteem was at an all-time low and I often felt worthless.

It's really sad to think back to who I was – but I am also deeply proud of the courage and trust that younger version of me had to take the first step and keep going.

Since stopping drinking, I feel more and more like the real 'me' inside. I haven't had anxiety in years, I do what I say I am going to, I put myself out there, I actually love myself, and on a practical level, I have written books and created an oracle card deck, re-launched my business, created magical offerings, and it's just getting better. Of course, this journey is layered, and it's not only down to stopping drinking alcohol that I am who I am today, but it certainly has played a big part in my journey.

I share this story to illustrate the shedding of layers that we have built up because they are what seems normal, or just how life is, but in fact, inside we know they are not for us and are actually stopping us from stepping into our full potential.

EMBODIED WEALTH PROMPTS

- *Is there anything you are being called to let go of right now?*
- *What one step can you take to let go or support yourself to do this?*

SECTION 3: HOLDING & SUPPORT

This section includes some ways to support yourself to move through anything that might be rising that's holding you back or stopping you from fully claiming your authentic power and embodying wealth.

BELONGING

Sometimes, in fact, most often, I don't know where I belong.
I belong to our great Mama Earth.
I belong to my body I have been gifted with.
I belong to the family and parents who have been with me for some or all of my journey.
I belong to the people who have touched my life, inspired and influenced me.
I belong to the Cosmos, the far-fetched corners of the Universe.
I belong to the memories and fields of consciousness that dance within my reality.
I also belong nowhere.
I am but a stitch in the tapestry of time.
A fleeting moment that is gone with a wisp of wind.
The twinkle of a star in a galaxy-filled sky.
I feel like I belong everywhere and nowhere all at the same time.
As I ponder my existence, my space within it all.
I know for sure that I am me.
And that is where I will always find that I belong.

Feeling like you belong is integral to this journey of becoming more and more you. Of being the most you that you can possibly be. Perhaps you find and feel belonging amongst others, a group, a family, an other, a community. Maybe it's simply feeling and knowing that you belong to yourself.

RADICAL SELF-CARE

I used to cater to everyone else but me. I couldn't be seen as lazy, selfish, or un-helpful if someone wanted or needed something, or I even remotely felt the heavy burden of expectation. Everyone and everything else came first.

I thought gym-ing with a personal trainer, and eating salads year round, even in the depths of a UK winter, was the way to go. I had no idea what I actually liked or what felt good in my body, or what my own needs were. I just went along with all the things I thought were right for me, and would get frustrated when I still didn't feel as amazing as the poster pin-ups looked like they did.

On top of the confusion around how to look after myself, I also had many underlying emotional issues around my own self-worth and self-esteem, so at the crux of it, I didn't feel I even deserved to be looked after. This was mirrored in my own self-abusive behaviour of binging and boozing, and completely numbing any feelings that were trying to be felt through other patterns and addictions. I share some of this journey in my first book, *Embodied*.

Even when I had done a lot of work on this and started to actually care about myself, I realised it was only the beginning! It's not just something you do to feel good about yourself once, and that's it – box ticked. It's actually choosing yourself over and over again, and as you do this, you begin to truly own your authentic power, which ripples out into all areas of your life and those you come into contact with.

It's a journey that evolves and grows as you do, based on your individual needs, what you are stepping into, and who you are becoming. I find that we need even more self-care – which is why I call it radical self-care – the more we align with our fullest potential.

At the end of the day, it often comes back down to basics, and I see it very much as the rooting and foundation for us to then spread our branches. Just like a seed spends time underground before it begins to sprout, we too need to shore up our grounding and base, so that we can grow in a strong and sustainable way.

Here are a few daily non-negotiable things that are my current go-to practices.

- Nervous system support, which might include calming and restorative yoga, taking supplements, breathwork, meditation, and time spent in nature.
- Basic foundations of self-care, which include sufficient rest, water, eating mostly fruits and vegetables, and moving your body regularly in a variety of ways.
- Setting a 40-day intention to guide your daily practice. This is something that you are focusing on that you want to bring more of (or less of, perhaps) into your life. For example, a recent one for me was 'Limitlessness'. Every day, I would tune into the intention and see what wanted to come. Some days I would journal on the word, others I would be led to watch or read something that would inspire me, sometimes it might show me the ways in which I felt the exact opposite. It kept me tuning into my own limitlessness, and after the 40 days, I definitely felt much more aligned with it and open to new ways. I am sure that there are also subtle shifts and changes still happening under the surface.
- Deep grounding and earthing, as above all, we are here on Earth having a physical experience. I also feel that being safe and held are key to inner wealth. This practice can include anything from a visualisation where I connect to the Earth Codes, merging them with my body, to simply lying or putting my feet on the ground.

Of course, there are many other things one can do. The point is that self-care and deeply honouring and listening to your body-mind-and-soul's needs are essential to being all you truly are here to be.

EMBODIED WEALTH PROMPT

- *What act of radical self-care is calling you right now?*

LET YOURSELF BE HELD

Lean into the support of all that is there, seen and unseen, felt and simply known.
Let it be there for you to find solace and sanctuary in.
As you let yourself surrender into its holding and strength, you create the space to welcome in your truth.

Allowing it to unfurl.
Explore and dance at its edges.
Playing with its facets.
Exploring its shadows.
Being all it wants to be.
Being all that it is.

Let yourself be held.

EMBODIED WEALTH SHARE

Recently I have deeply felt the need for more masculine holding support. For me, this comes in the form of a male person, but it is also about the masculine energy on a deeper level. I realise, looking over my life, that I don't trust the masculine to hold me. All of me. I have been abandoned and rejected in almost all of my intimate relationships, and my relationship with my father was tumultuous and felt un-safe for a lot of my childhood (which I share more about in my first book, *Embodied*).

I know that I haven't ever fully let myself be held by the masculine; in fact, it felt too much for a long time, and I expected it not to be there. So I have consciously been feeling into the energy of the masculine and allowing myself to soften to it. To feel held by it, to welcome it in. Imagining myself leaning into it and seeing me fully. I also am choosing to work with male healers (that feel aligned) at this point in time, to soften to this energy in the physical.

It's such a powerful practice which is supporting me to feel more safe to be me.

EMBODIED WEALTH PROMPT

- *How can you open to the support available to you in all forms and lean into it more? Trust what comes to you now.*

HOW GOOD CAN YOU ALLOW IT TO GET?

To begin to embody wealth in all areas of your life, start from within and acknowledge where you are at right now. A powerful question to begin to do this is asking, 'How good can you allow it to get?'

Often we say we want one thing, but when it comes down to it, we can't actually receive it, due to all the beliefs and conditioning we have got going on sub- or un-consciously.

We can't allow it to be *that* good. We just can't receive it.

Guilt, shame, judgements, or something else might begin to surface, which stop us from allowing it to be *that* good. So many people are suffering, struggling, living hard lives – and again, I deeply acknowledge the systems that we have been born into, which literally thrive by keeping this as the status quo – that we don't want to be seen as having it easy, joyful, or something else.

We may have ancestral or other traumas, fears, and beliefs that we are carrying, which are held in our bodies through the lineages, and these stop us from allowing it to be good, on multiple levels. Perhaps your ancestors lost everything, so there's a fear of allowing things to come in, just in case that happens again. These things often aren't conscious – they are hidden in our bodies, in our memories, in our energy fields.

But we can't embody our wealth, power, and truth, and begin to change the world for all if we can't allow it to be as good as it can be on an individual level.

EMBODIED WEALTH PRACTICE

I invite you to write a list of all the main areas in your life – e.g. home, relationships, health, finances, career, family, free time, personal growth, spirituality, etc. You can refer back to the exercise in the first section, 'Activating wealth in your life'. For each one, answer the following questions:

- *How would it feel to have all that you desire in this area?*
- *Is there anything coming up in you that can't receive it? That can't allow it to be that good? What thoughts are rising? Spend some time really allowing what wants to come up here, and you may find you come back and add to it, as things 'pop' throughout your day.*
- *How does it feel to acknowledge this?*
- *How could you support yourself to let this go? There is support for this later on.*

As the mind often comes up with reasons why you can't allow it to be that good, the body may also have stored information for you too. There's some support with this in the next two pieces inviting you to dive more deeply into your body. I also always recommend reaching out to someone you trust who can guide and support you, especially as there might be deep and traumatic things that rise.

Take it further by feeling into these prompts. Let the words sit with you, feel them in your body, and perhaps journal on them, seeing what they bring up.

- *Can you let yourself receive all that wants to come to you?*
- *Can you let yourself own your gifts and talents?*
- *Can you let yourself step into your power?*
- *Can you let yourself be all you can be?*

THE WEALTH OF WISDOM IN OUR BODIES

The wisdom of our bodies is something that I probably will always be passionate about as it has played such a significant part in my life here on Earth, both personally and in my work with others. It took me 'leaving' my body and numbing and avoiding every sign and signal it gave me, to finding my way back and forming a magical connection with it.

Establishing this deep connection with every part of my physical body, and tuning into its guidance and wisdom, is something that blows my mind every time I allow the space and time for it. There truly is unlimited wealth in our bodies.

Our bodies tell us when something is off or isn't right for us.
Our bodies tell us when to slow down and when we need to rest.
Our bodies are our homes, and they want to do their best to hold each of us on our journey. All they ask in return is that you care for them and give them nourishment, movement, and rest – and even when we don't, they are pretty resilient!

So many of us neglect our bodies. We don't feed and water them when the signs are there, we don't let them sleep, we push them too hard, and we give them things that spike adrenaline and cause other imbalances. So they start to scream at us – the pains, the hurts, the aches, all getting louder – and we enter into a relationship akin to a caged animal whose natural instinctual needs are totally ignored, with our beautiful bodies.

But, when we truly listen to our bodies, each and every part, we begin to see how they have always been on our side – they are simply mirroring where and what the issue is that is rising for you, so that it can be held and supported.

I have to give Louise Hay the utmost credit, as her list of symptoms according to body parts in her book *You Can Heal Your Life* is incredible. I use it whenever I feel a part of my body calling me.

It is so spot on with the emotional/other reasons why you might be feeling a physical symptom, which then means you can support and hold yourself (or get help) to move through whatever is calling for attention.

For example, I suddenly had a pain in my elbow for no apparent reason, and the elbow, according to Louise Hay, is all about changing direction and accepting new experiences. This totally resonated as I was literally preparing to move countries and begin an adventure travelling for a bit before finding my next home, and I was definitely feeling some apprehension about it all. Just knowing this gave me a sense of peace, and I was able to journal and sit with myself, honouring that I was feeling some nervousness, which I had been previously ignoring. As a result I felt better overall and the elbow pain went almost instantly!

Our bodies are such magnificent allies on this journey, always calling us back home to ourselves, guiding us to true wealth.

Deep diving into the body

For the past few years, I have been guiding people into their bodies. Into the parts that might feel fear, anxiety, sadness, un-worthiness – the parts that are calling for attention. Rather than avoiding these parts as we have been taught to do, they are, in fact, where the wealth lies.

These parts are calling out to us to pay attention. They are the parts that have messages for us; the parts which might simply need acknowledgement; where something is un-resolved; where we have created a belief that isn't serving us; where there is holding and healing needed.

As we sit with them, listen to them, feel them, hold them, and let them guide us, we find peace, joy, love, release, and a letting go which enables us to become more and more aligned with our truth.

EMBODIED WEALTH PRACTICE

I invite you to regularly tune into your body and notice where it is trying to speak to you. Which part is feeling something? Take a moment to ask it if it has anything it would like to share with you, being open to the answer.

Embodied Wealth share: A journaling conversation with myself

'What's going on today? What's rising?'

I don't matter. There isn't time for me. My needs, feelings, and time can be brushed aside or put back. If I need some support, energy or attention, I have to pay for it, but others don't. I come second. I have to abandon myself for others. I have felt abandoned in relationships, and abandoned in general.

I also abandon myself through addictive patterns and behaviours, so I don't have to feel anything, or so I can feel a 'high' that's not natural.

Being left (or abandoned) by three parents – two biological and one adopted who passed on – makes me feel like I'm not enough and it's okay to abandon and reject me. I have had this mirrored throughout my life.

'I'm so sorry you feel and have felt this. What do you need?'

I need to let this go. I hold myself deeply, I let myself release and feel all that needs to be felt. I notice it and acknowledge the pattern. I choose for it to end now as this is not what I want in my life moving forward.

As I looked into it more deeply, I asked: 'Where am I abandoning and rejecting myself? What is this part or parts that I don't accept? Who is she? What is she?'

My light, my essence, my power, my life-force, my internal flame that I dimmed and haven't tended to. The me that takes no BS, that speaks up, speaks her mind, is not afraid, and is more powerful than I could ever imagine.

'How can you welcome these parts, her, into your life again? How do you embrace her as a part of your wholeness?'

Connect with her, hold her, tell her I love her. I am so sorry for abandoning and rejecting you. I welcome you and commit to embodying you.

THE GIFTS OF YOUR ANCESTRY

What are the gifts of your ancestry and heritage that you would like to experience and embody as you step into your power?

Whilst there are many beliefs, programmes, and conditioning that we have taken on in our lineages that do not serve us, there are many things that do add to the wealth of our lives.

There are threads of wisdom; qualities and behaviours; stories which create connection and grounding; innate skills and gifts; a depth of richness and experiences which truly can support you in embodying all you are here to be.

This might be something you can actually research, looking into your family history and letting what inspires and intrigues you be your guide for what you might explore.

Or you could simply trust the sparks of ideas and inspiration that you are called to dive into, calling on your ancestors to guide and hold you on your journey.

For example, you might be called to cook something from another culture or country. You might want to try painting using a certain technique. Maybe you are being called to volunteer and help in a certain part of the world.

SECTION 4: CLAIMING YOUR I AM

THE COLOURS OF WEALTH

Colour has always played a huge part in my life, and in my opinion is one of the most powerful tools for showing us hidden blocks, stories, patterns, and behaviours that we are still holding on to, stopping us from fully stepping into all that we are, our wholeness, and our truth.

In this section, you will find stories, journeys, past-life regressions, inspiration, ideas and ways to support you to embody wealth (aligning more and more with your true self) in every area of your life. Each piece within this section has been inspired by or come from my work with colour and colour combinations, including many of the bottles in the Colour Mirrors system.

Colour Mirrors is a system (of coloured bottles of oils and essences) that tunes into the power of colour as a mirror for what is going on inside. The colours (and combinations) that you are drawn to and repelled by can reveal where there might be healing needed, as well as show your talents, gifts, and more.

To illustrate, when I first began working with the colour gold, I had a migraine and was bed-bound in serious pain for three days. I literally couldn't do anything. Then in the days that followed, I experienced lots of triggers around me stepping up into what I was being called into, stepping into my power, which came up in all areas of my life, from work to seemingly meaningless interactions.

Then as I began to go into it to hold and acknowledge what was rising, I experienced some deep healing around past lives in Atlantis and Egypt. Sometimes you don't even realise what's coming up, but colour has this magical way of bringing up what you need to release – it truly is an activator. It can then also be used as the balm or remedy to hold you through what's rising.

To begin, I recommend bringing your awareness to an issue that might be rising for you, or for something you would like guidance on, then asking yourself which colour would support you with it.

Then I invite you to choose a message/story/piece of guidance from that section, trusting that it's what you need to receive in this moment.

Or you could simply ask, 'What do I need to know right now?' then pick a colour or story intuitively from the contents page. Another way you can use this section is to pick a colour that seems to be in your awareness a lot (whether that's because you are attracted to it, or repelled by it), then see what the messages are. Always do what resonates for you and if you want to use it in another way, do that. You can't get this wrong!

The colours included are:
- Copper
- Red
- Pink
- Coral
- Orange
- Gold
- Yellow
- Olive
- Green
- Turquoise
- Blue
- Indigo
- Violet
- Magenta
- Lilac
- White

There are also some further resources in the end if you would like to dive into colour alchemy more deeply.

COPPER

Body wisdom

Your body is integral to your journey here on earth.
There is no separation between you and your body while you are
here.
Take the time to really feel it, be with it, listen to it, and receive it.

It carries deep nuggets of wisdom that you might need for this
journey.
It holds ancient truths that can support you.
Let it lead you, let it show you, let it be a guiding compass for your
way.

Feel its strength.
Feel its wisdom.
Feel its beauty.
Feel its power.

Love your body, and in return, it will show you your way.

Heart power

I felt my legs and arms burning as I was being pulled deeper and deeper underground. Sweat was dripping down my back, my forehead, my neck. I felt drenched as my body tumbled and turned, going downwards.

I landed in a vast cavern, the sound of machines clanking and slamming. The air was sticky and thick with the pungent smell of sweat. As my eyes adjusted to the fogginess, the space came more into focus. I saw rows and rows of slaves working the machines – which all seemed to be fuelling a golden orb-like structure in the centre. I saw a man overseeing it all from a high-up balcony, shouting orders when he saw something 'out of line'. He seemed defeated and broken; there was a deep sense of sadness in his eyes.

The scene moved ahead, and I found myself in a room directly beneath the golden orb. Its base filled the ceiling, and from it were hundreds of tentacles of golden light, each coming off and attaching to a different switch on this giant machine. The switches were each labelled in some kind of code, and it was making a humming sound with the occasional crackle.

Suddenly the man I had seen came into the room, panting. Gasping for air, he said, 'They are coming for me, quickly listen...

'Don't give away your power so easily, just because you don't know how to use it, or fear using it for control or to hurt someone. Don't let others take your power by feeding into their systems of control. It's so easy to let that happen when you get caught up in the fear.

'Remember the power is already inside of you. It may feel like you need a key to unlock it, but you don't. Lean into the power of your heart and let that guide you. That is your true power. You don't need to fear falling back into patterns of power over someone, as long as you lean into your heart.

Now is the time to use your power for the highest good. For love, for creation, togetherness, support, empathy, compassion, beauty, and for change.'

With that, the man was taken away by the guards, and the scene moved on almost instantly. I found myself in a giant womb-like space, immersed in a sea of pink plasma. I knew I was ready to be re-born.

Let go

Let go.
Let go.
Let go.

Stop holding on so tightly.
Stop trying to control.

Let go.
Let go.
Let go.

When you try to hold on and control.
You leave a little piece of yourself in that moment.

Let go.
Let go.
Let go.

You might feel scattered and all over the place.
Un-grounded and not in your wholeness.

Let go.
Let go.
Let go.

Imagine each piece a glistening jewel.
Calling them back, one by one.

Let go.
Let go.
Let go.

As you release your grip, surrender your hold.
You will find sanctuary in the cocoon of your truth.

Journey into the heart of the Earth

I found myself on a boat in a dark cave, with someone behind me rowing, I didn't need to know who it was. The waters were gently lapping beneath the oars as I was taken deeper into the cave. Suddenly fireflies appeared everywhere, lighting our way, as we went further and further within. I felt calm, peaceful, cocooned in the Great Mother.

We travelled for a while before arriving at a portal, where the waters started to cascade downwards; it was a waterfall that led right into the heart of the Earth. I was asked whether I wanted to go. I replied yes, and before I knew it, I was moving through the portal, flying at lightning speed, down, down, down.

I landed in an opening, and as I looked up and around, I began to take in the most luscious space I have ever seen. Trees, flowers, plants, of all shapes, colours and sizes, dancing in unison, swaying along with the gentle breeze. There were water pools with lily pads of all sizes and multi-coloured fish shimmering beneath the surface. There were piles of crystals scattered everywhere, and the skies appeared to be a deep blue one minute, then the most beautiful sunset the next.

The air was deeply nourishing, and I could feel my body softening into its hold. This was the land of abundance, wealth, and possibility.

I wondered where to go next, and a guide was instantly by my side, taking my hand, leading me to one side of a mountain, down a winding path that towered above the fertile lands. We kept on walking until we got to a round field, and almost as quickly, it was dark and I could see star constellations, multiple milky ways, even planets were distinctly visible, each with their unique characteristics – colours, moons, and varying sizes. It was all there.

Staring up at the vastness of the Cosmos from the heart of the Earth, I felt the richness and beauty of it all. I felt how the stars guided our ancestors and still do for some groups of people and tribes today. I felt how the earth is our guide whilst we are here. How the guidance is always there, within. Our bodies are a mirror for it all. They contain the wisdom of the night sky, and the heart is the guiding North Star. Our bodies are like the soils of the Earth, ready to be tilled and seeds planted.

We have all we need to create wealth, abundance, beauty, joy, whatever we desire.
But we have to remember that first.

When it feels too much

Sometimes being on Earth can be SO much. It can feel so overwhelming, so painful, so unfair. There's so much struggle, so much hatred, so much war, so much that is out of control, it feels futile.
You might often wonder why you're here. Is it even worth it?

I get it. So many of us get it and can feel this way. You are not alone.

But you are so needed at this time.

Hold yourself as you feel it, hold yourself deeply through it all.
Look after your vessel – your wise, beautiful body as best you can, to support you on your journey.
Keep showing up in the ways you are being called to.
Connect with the Earth and let her hold you when it all feels too much.
Find community and support that resonate in your heart.

You are so needed at this time.

RED

Experience more

Money is a tool to receive more of what your soul came here to experience.

Why would you ever deny it that?

It's time to start stepping into the wealth of life. The wonderful experiences of this planet – travel, adventure, excitement, connection. All that you desire to have and feel in your life.

Money is simply (but powerfully) a conduit for that. It is not the only way – you can skip ahead straight to the experience – but it is a way to experience.

I invite you to welcome in money as a friend, a support, a being that wants to help you live a more full, rich, and expansive life, filled with experiences.

EMBODIED WEALTH SHARE

Once I had this realisation that just clicked on another level, I felt a shift in my relationship with money, and I wrote this journal entry:

Dear Money,
I get it. I get your purpose, your energy. What you have been trying to tell me all along.
I feel like something has just clicked, and I am in the vortex of your field. The codes are now unlocked and we are one. You have been trying to get to me all along, and I don't even want to go into why I didn't, or wouldn't, let you in. But I feel you now. I get how spiritual you actually are. How integral a part of what it means to have a human experience. I feel so incredibly blessed. This feels like a huge awakening, and I am now in the portal of the next chapter of my life. I thank you for being a part of this journey with me. I thank you for coming to me in the most magical ways, expected and unexpected, for the highest good of all.

I thank you for being a part of all that I will experience and have already experienced, and I am so excited for our growing, deepening relationship. Money. You are freaking awesome. Let's begin our new relationship from now. I love you. Thank you.

The mirror

What if everything you see, hear, and experience is a mirror for what is going on inside – collectively and individually?

What if the Earth's pollution is a mirror for the toxicity we embody collectively?
What if the pain and suffering we see is a mirror for what's going on inside of the majority?
What if the prevalent consumer culture is a mirror for how we are desperately trying to fill ourselves up?
What if the more extreme weather conditions we now experience are mirroring the suppression of our truth that is reaching a boiling point?
What if the increase in diseases is showing us the increase in diseases we now carry on all levels – emotionally, mentally and physically?

It starts with one person. It starts with you.

What do you need to feel more safe, grounded, and held?
What ignites your creative fire?
What fills you up on a deep and meaningful level?
What opens your heart?
What connects you with a deeper purpose?
What makes you feel connected to a greater vision for us all?

Start here, start with you.
Then let this energy spill over.

What is your 'no'?

Having a clear and powerful 'no' is just as important as your 'yes'. When you say 'no' to something, you open space for a 'yes' to something else. You open space for a 'yes' to yourself and what is truly aligned with who you are.

This is something that can be hard for many as we have been conditioned to people please, to put others' needs first, to not want to make anyone else feel uncomfortable, or hurt their feelings in any way.

Fuck that shit!

It's time to assert your boundary and your 'no'. Get to know YOU. Do you really want it? Is it a full-body 'yes'? Is it something that serves you? Is it something that lights you up? Is it something that will expand you? Is it something that will nourish you?

Of course, I acknowledge that this might be a journey, and maybe there are some things that you just have to say 'yes' to for the moment (like at work), but what are you saying 'yes' to that you don't really want and will end up resenting, wishing you had said 'no' to?

Say 'no' or 'Can I get back to you?' – so you can really feel into something, before saying 'yes' to things that are asked of you.

Owning your *shiz*

Do you own your power?
Do you own your vulnerability?
Do you own your gifts?
Do you own your potential?
Do you own your shadow?
Do you own your fears?
Do you own your journey?
Do you own who YOU are?

It is time to own the shit out of who you are.

Where are you settling?

You know it in your heart where you are settling for less.
Saying 'yes' to something that isn't aligned.
Putting up with something that isn't worth your energy.

Yes, there may be times and experiences where there is a higher lesson or learning for you.
But if you are honest with yourself, you know where you are settling for less.

What are you afraid will happen if you say 'no'?
What do you fear losing if you assert that boundary?
What bad thing do you think will happen if you let go?

Take the time to hold and honour, then release all the fears rising.

It's time to say 'no'.
It's time to put yourself first.
It's time to let go.

⑨INK

Gentle power

There's power in your softness.
There's power in your gentleness.
There's power in your peaceful nature.

There's power in your compassion.
There's power in your empathy.
There's power in your holding.

There's power in the way you reflect.
There's power in how you really see others.
There's power in the way you are.

This is the power the world so badly needs.
This is the power that you are.

Rose pink

All day I was craving the colour rose pink without even realising it. On my morning walk, the rose pink bougainvillaea popped, catching my attention, and I just had to gather a few fallen flowers to keep by my side all day. I had eaten the pink-coloured foods I had in my kitchen (raspberries and red grapes). Later, when I looked down at what I was wearing, I noticed almost rose-pink trousers and a deep rose scarf.

Then it caught my attention – I had been drawn to rose pink all day.

There was something about the colour that felt comforting, softening, soothing and deeply supportive. At the time of writing, I was getting ready to go back to the UK after more than two years away. A lot of stuff was rising, and the threads of fear were making themselves known: What was next? Where would I live? Did I have all the requirements for travel? How did I feel about it all? Did I want to go back?

So I asked rose pink to hold me and show me the way through. I had a rose-pink essence that had also been calling for my attention, so I poured some into a bath. later adding some dried rose petals, which I deeply immersed myself in.

As I let myself be held by the rose-pink energy, I felt the fears, the anxieties, the mind chatter melting off my body and into the water. My back softened into the warmth, and I felt a rush of love and support all around me.

I began a journey into rose pink...

I felt four Marys – my own mum who was called Mary, Mary Magdalene, Mother Mary, and someone called Mary Rose, on all sides of me. Their arms holding me, showing me I am always supported.

I was taken down a winding tree-lined pathway until, up ahead, we reached an opening. There were rose bushes on all sides, and the space turned into a courtyard with fairy lights twinkling above.

I felt a rush of warmth and love, and the energy of someone I don't yet know. Someone who will play a significant part in my life. Someone who will open my heart even more.

As I felt the beauty, love, and sheer perfection of this moment, I heard the message, 'Sometimes you have to take journeys and follow the winding path into the unknown to create a life of love. Just remember you are always held and supported.'

I was reminded that I am stepping into the next part of my journey and adventure in this magical life I get to live. Rose pink brought me back to that knowing and truth.

The child inside

What if you could see the child inside every person?
What if you could see all that they had been through?
Why they are the way they are.
Why they act out. Recoil. Lash out.

What if you could see their innocence, their love, and their truth?
It's just been hidden under layers of conditioning, influence, stories,
pain, beliefs, and life.

What would you feel, think, say, know about them now?
Remember, you are that child too.

The golden egg

In the vision, I was travelling down a trail in the forest until I came across a solid golden egg. As well as not letting me touch it, it was blocking the way forward, and every time I tried to get near or go around it, it moved. I could see beyond it was a life filled with things I desired. But I couldn't get to it.

I then heard the words, 'You have got to choose it, and let yourself receive it.' It was reminding me that I hold on to stories, beliefs, blocks, and patterns, and often I don't let myself have what I desire for one reason or another. So, I declared that I choose it, feeling it deep within my core, and then I saw the golden egg begin to dissolve. As it melted away, it took with it the resistance, the barriers, the walls, the heaviness, the sludge, and the stories. Letting them go, with ease, simply by choosing.

The scene then turned into a plain white room, a blank canvas if you will. It asked me, 'What do you want to create today?'

CORAL

Deep holding

One moment I was below the surface of the earth, burrowing like a rabbit in its lair, the next I was off in the galaxies sliding on the rings of Jupiter, flying, leaping, expanding into my great-ness.

I felt the power of being held, deeply accepted, loved and nurtured and how it's the grounding and rooting for allowing yourself to expand.

So many of us don't feel safe to be held and supported, let alone loved and nurtured, as often we weren't as children, so don't know how to receive it.

This is the key to expanding into your great-ness, and starts with you.
Hold yourself.
Support yourself.
Love yourself.
Nurture yourself.

Then begin to ask for it from others, the unseen and wherever you are called to.

Half in and half out

Do you have one foot on the ground and one wanting to not be here?
Have you fully landed here on Earth, or are you half in and half out?

One of the most life-changing things I have ever done is committing to be here on Earth fully. To be here with all that life brings. Every experience, every moment. All of it.

To let myself surrender into my body. Into the holding of Mother Earth. Into myself.

When I fully declared this, I felt a cord attached from my belly button going down into the heart of the Earth. One then also attached to the back of my head and went upwards, connecting to the cosmic womb.

I know how held and connected I am to both the Cosmos and Earth.

My body feels so much

I wonder sometimes if I am too much.
I need so much gentle-ness.
So much alone time.
So much rest.

When I try to live in the same way as the majority, I find the irritation bubbling, the agitation surfacing. I wonder if I'm doing something wrong. How can I live and be more like others?

I despair that the world isn't built for the extreme sensitivity I experience. I hear every single noise, I feel the vibrations in my bones. I notice acute shifts in the weather. I feel the energy of people and objects around me.

I feel the tears bubbling when it's all been too much. When I finally get a moment alone, a moment to let go, they come streaming in relief. It's like my body holds everything it takes in, through all of the senses, and then it needs to let go.

The only way through is next-level, radical, non-negotiable, daily self-care.

Care for my body.
Compassion for my body.
Nurturing my body.
Listening to my body.
Being in my body.
Parenting my body.
Loving my body.

Receiving ALL of you

Do you receive your cosmic self?
Do you receive your human self?
Do you receive the parts that are messy?
Do you receive the parts that are your gifts?

The parts that come easily to you.
The parts that sparkle and shine.
The parts that may have been called 'too much'.
The parts that are loud, big and bold.
The parts that are fierce and don't give a fuck.
The parts that are gentle and soft.
The parts that are sexy and inviting.

Do you feel safe to receive all of you?

ORANGE

Bring the love

What if you could bring love to everything?
To every experience you get to have, no matter the outcome.
To every person you come into contact with, no matter the exchange.
To everything you get to see, hear and feel, no matter how it's received.
To each moment of your life as it unfolds, no matter how painful, difficult, or challenging.
To always bring love.

What might that be like?

Let it burn

The flames engulfed me, my body burning. Everything that wasn't mine, everything I no longer needed, all the stories and conditioning that aren't supportive, all the shit, was taken into the flames, to be burned to the ground.

Then I saw this open land – dry and desolate, it too had been burned away. As I looked more closely, I realised it was fertile soil, ready to be tilled and nourished for new growth, for a new way, for beauty and love.

But first, we must let the old go. Let it burn away.

Then we can plant the seeds of new desires. Seeds for what you choose to now grow.

You are a destroyer.
You are a creator.
You get to choose what you grow.

Portals

Think of what you desire to be, embody, or become as a portal. Also akin to a vortex, or energy field, that you can simply step into.

You might like to see it as a swirling energy of colour that holds a unique vibration, essence, and feeling that is unique to it, that you can feel/see/hear/touch. As you get closer to it and begin to embody it, you start to mirror this vibration in your body and bring what you desire closer to you in the physical.

EMBODIED WEALTH PRACTICE

Take a moment to play with a portal. You might like to close your eyes and visualise. Or perhaps you prefer to create what you experience, or speak it out loud.

Imagine yourself stepping into the portal of 'Pleasure'. Call in the word, and let it be felt in your body.

What does it feel like?

Now I invite you to step into the portal of 'Power'. Calling in the word, let it wash into your body.

What does this one feel like?

Now I invite you to step into the portal of 'Wealth'. Feel the energy of the word, let it wash into your body.

What does this one feel like?

Now I invite you to step into the portal of what you are choosing.

Phoenix rising

There's an anger bubbling.
It's getting louder, stronger, bolder.
Until it comes out as rage.
Pure fucking rage.

Why are we in this situation?
Why has it got to this point?
How have we let it get here?
All the questions, the fury, the demand for answers.

Then comes the blame.
It's the masculine. The patriarchy.
It's got us to this point.
It can't hold the feminine.
In fact, it has hurt it, and demonised it.
It can't be with it, let alone honour it.
Let it be its full glorious self.
So it has shied away, felt un-grounded and un-held.
Not let itself out.

But.

What if we stopped all the blame and shame?
Remember, we all carry both of these energies inside.
You are the holding of the masculine with the flowing of the feminine.
The inspiration of the feminine with the grounded action of the masculine.
It's your responsibility to welcome in and get to know both.
Each in their varying amounts and qualities, unique to you.

Let's burn down that separation and old-paradigm way.
Claim back our wholeness.
Hold ourselves fully.
There's a phoenix that wants to rise, from within.

GOLD

Hard work

There's a part inside of me that believes it has to be hard work. You have to earn, strive, work hard, or prove yourself to bring in the good life. As I connected more deeply with this part, it felt like it was fearful of some power, master, or overlord, who wanted to see it struggle and always be working and doing. This was the only acceptable way. This is how it was.

It felt absolutely shattered and almost frozen in this paradigm.

Asking it what it needed, it said, 'Rest'. Lots of rest. So I imagined taking it to a luxury hotel where it was pampered, where it got to sleep in the softest cotton sheets, take a glorious bubble bath to soothe its aching muscles, and be left alone to replenish.

As it did this, fear of judgement from others still came up, fear that it would get into trouble, fear it would get caught or found out for not working hard. There were also threads of guilt that it got to rest when others didn't.

It felt like an ancestral belief and conditioning, intertwined with a patriarchal, capitalist mentality, that has been passed along for centuries, that it is now time to let go of. It's time to welcome in ease. Time to welcome in a new way. Time to show others that it is possible to do it in a new way.

I held the part in a mothering rose-gold light, which began to melt away the fear. It began to soften into this possibility and potential of allowing it to be easy, allowing it to feel good, allowing it to honour its needs.

Why do we overcomplicate it?
Feel and think it has to be so hard?
Why do we have to strive, push, force or struggle?
Before we can have what we desire?

Before we can let ourselves be all we can be?
Before we step into and embody our truth?
Where are you making it hard for yourself?

I AM

Where are you not claiming your power?
Where are you not claiming your truth?
Where are you not claiming your wholeness?
Where are you not claiming who YOU are?

Where are you shying away from your magnificence?
Where are you hiding from your unique qualities?
Where are you dulling your sparkle?
Where are you ignoring the whispers of your soul?

It is time.
It is time.
It is time.
Time to...

Step into it.
Claim it.
Live it.
Be it.
I AM...

Your dear body

We hold so much in our bodies.
Every hurt, every pain, every memory and more.
It carries it all as our faithful companion.
It holds on to it deep within our core.

So when we begin to make changes.
Step into our power, our wisdom, our truth.
The body might need extra holding and support.
So it too can begin to align with this way.

It may need holding to release old patterns.
It may need movement to let go.
It may need gentleness and rest to integrate.
It may need extra nourishment to ground more deeply.

Be extra compassionate and kind to your dear body.
Hold space for it to receive what it needs.
Remember it takes a little more time.
So be patient with it as it begins to align.

Rise in your power

There's a place of deep peace and stillness.
It's grounded, rooted, embodied and whole.
There is no fear here.
No competition.
No stress and no anxiety.
It's like the depths of the ocean.
The bed of the forest.
The vastness of the night sky.
It carries all of your potential.
Deeply sees and knows you.
It calls on you to come from this place.
To connect to and merge with it.
Be still here for a moment.
Then you can truly rise in your power.

YELLOW

Stuck in the head

Where are you in your head too much?
Where have you been over-thinking or analysing things too much?
Where have you been trying to control an outcome or situation?
Where can you get support and hand some of the things on your to-do list over to someone else?

We are not meant to be in our heads as much as most of us are. This is an invitation to get out of your head and into your body, in whatever way calls you right now.

You are all of it

The sun shines down upon you.
The grass is beneath your feet.
Your body is held and nourished by this golden yellow and green energy.
Take a moment to breathe it in.
Deep into your core.

You are all of it.
The beaming power of the sun.
The strength and grounding of the earth.
This is your truth.
Your I AM.
Take a moment to breathe it in.
Deep into your core.

The wonder in wealth

When I was a child, I made every experience magical. I saw the opportunity for wealth in each moment.

The pillows strategically placed on the living room floor were islands you had to hop to and from to escape the crocodiles (AKA the person named 'it' who could come and get you) eating you, if you touched the floor. But on those pillows, you were invincible to everything.

Juicy pomegranates fresh from the tree were an elixir from the Goddess, and you received magical powers with every bursting mouthful, red juice dripping down your chin – which you quickly scooped up so as not to miss out on any of the potent powers.

The minute my little body entered the swimming pool, I became a mermaid under the waters, and I would invite friends down for underwater tea in my coral and crystal palace, as I was ruler of the oceans.

Wandering around the garden, no matter where or what country, I would find little spots the fairies had left behind to find sanctuary in. Tree creatures, elves, and other magical beings were my friends, and we lived in harmony with one another.

I knew that life was deeply magical, abundant, over-flowing and mystical, and I could be anybody and anything I wanted. I was limitless.

OLIVE

Just be you

Who are YOU here to be?

What is your truth?

What is your power?

What is your essence?

What is unique to you?

You didn't come here to be anyone else.

Sometimes, or maybe a lot of the time, this journey can feel so lonely. Like you don't fit in or belong. You may be faced with situations and people who are different to you. Where you feel that difference so strongly. Feel like an outsider from another planet.

But this is your invitation to lean into you.
Your background, your story, your upbringing, your life.
Your strengths and your shadows.

All of this is what makes you, you.
That is who you came here to be.
So, just be you.

Connect to your power

There's a part inside of you.
Maybe it's a few.
It's where you dis-owned yourself.
As you thought you were too much.

Too sexy.
Too loud.
Too bold.
Too boundaried.
Too YOU, in some way.

It wasn't acceptable.
Others didn't like it.
It didn't fit in.
So you shut it in a box, and buried or threw it away.

But this is a part of you.
An integral part of your wholeness.
It's a part that completes you.
Connects you to your power.

Now is the time to remember and reclaim it.
To welcome it back.
To embody it.
To own it.

This part will support you to step into your power.
This part of you is needed to be ALL you are here to be.
As you claim your full self.
You truly can own your power

You are here to show others what's possible

You are here to show others what's possible.
Remind them of their power and potential.
Show them that we can live in a world where we honour each other – our strengths, our talents, our challenges, our truth, our differences, and our similarities.

You are here to show others what's possible.
As you step into more and more of yourself.
As you begin to step into your authentic leadership, which is about true honouring and nurturing of others.

You are here to show others what's possible.
As you let go of the old stories, ways, and conditioning.
To truly embody a way that we've been taught is not achievable without struggle, greed, and control over others.

You are here to show others what's possible.
A way where you get to be fully you.
A way that feels good in your body.
A way that is aligned with your gifts, your talents and strengths.
A way that works in consideration of others, for the good of all.
A way that is fuelled by love and joy.

GREEN

Craving space

I need a lot of space. For stillness, peace and time – to be with myself. My thoughts, my inner world, my connection to my creativity, space to simply be.

Often it can be hard to find this space I so deeply crave as the world is sometimes so loud, and overwhelming.

I was shown that I can always find space in pockets within my body. When I consciously decide to do a deep yin posture or stretch, I create the space I desire, and I can return to myself again.

Follow the body

Just as the stars guided the ancients, the body guides us today.
Your body is your guide and compass to create true wealth on YOUR terms.
Tune into your body and feel which part is calling you.
Then ask it what it would like to show you, and let yourself be guided.
Ask for your one next step, let it come to you in visions, sounds, a knowing, a feeling or perhaps another way.
It may not make sense. It may seem counterintuitive or illogical.
I invite you to trust it.
We are only ever given that next one step to take.
You'll need to let go of control, trying to plan ahead and figure it all out.
Just take that one next step.

The wisdom of nature

What flower, plant, or tree deeply calls to you?
What is its nature?
What is its unique essence?
When does it bloom?
Is it seasonal?
Is it evergreen?

There's wisdom in nature.
The way it's cyclical, seasonal, rhythmic.
The way it adapts to its environment and terrain.

How have you adapted to yours?
Do you honour yours?
Do you accept yours?
Or do you push against it, fight it, ignore it?

This is your invitation to deeply tune into the flower, plant, or tree that resonates most for you now. Let its qualities inspire and guide you. Let it be your muse. As it honours its needs, and invites you to honour yours too.

The emerald elixir

I landed in the body of a woman running for her life. Her bare feet were leaping over the rocks, the grass, the road, just to get away. Who from? I wasn't sure yet.

I looked down, my feet still moving fast, and I could see a velvet green dress, the bodice embroidered with some kind of symbols. My throat was dry, I held a hand up to my chest, it was burning as I tried to catch my breath.

Suddenly I felt *them* upon me. I had been caught.

A burly, hairy arm was pulling me back, and the next thing I knew, a sack had been placed over my head. My hands were tied behind my back, my feet were bound to one another, and I was thrown on the back of a cart. We began to move, and I could hear the wheels juddering against the rocks, the vibration reverberating throughout my body.

I knew that was it. I was a dead woman.

They had been trying to catch me for years as I had been making a remedy, 'the emerald elixir', from herbs and plants that grew in the region, to help people with their ailments. They didn't trust me and thought that I was a witch. I wasn't sure how they had found me this time but felt that someone had ratted me out. Someone had been turned by them.

I felt such a deep sense of sadness, anger, despair. What was going to happen to all the people I had been helping now? I thought about how I could escape, but the rope was tied so tight I could feel the blood pooling together in my limbs around it.

Suddenly the cart jolted to a holt. I heard the sound of muffled voices that felt fierce and assertive. Then the creak and bang of the door being opened, and I was being yanked out.

This was it, my end was near.

The rough cloth scratched as it was pulled from my head. My eyes squinted as the sun had risen, and it took a moment to adjust to what was going on in front of me.

Then I saw it, we were still on the edges of town, the trees were dense and there were dozens of people surrounding us with tools, knives, pitchforks, all pointed towards the two men that had grabbed me. I saw the faces of people I had helped. People who had been supported by the emerald elixir. I could see the compassion, support, determination, and love in their eyes.

'Let her go,' one of them instructed.

'We need her.'

TURQUOISE

Cave of abundance

I felt a wave of joy take over and immediately was taken back to when I was a child exploring the garden. A place where I felt so free and like anything was possible. There were colours everywhere, joy in the simple, magic in the unseen, having fun just by being alive. I was reminded that this is what really matters. This is true wealth to me.

The Goddess Lakshmi then came to me, taking me by the hand. She took me for a walk down a seashell-covered beach to a cave on one side of a little cove, its entrance slightly hidden by the lush, tropical overgrowth.

I went into it, with a deep knowing that this was a cave of abundance that could show me how to embody and bring about more of anything I desire or wish to experience. The first room I was shown was love, and I felt a soft pink colour begin to take over the room. Its gentle power holding me as I melted into its embrace. It softened my heart and told me I was safe and held.

The next room I was shown was joy, and I felt rays of sunshine streaming in, with the vibrant energy of yellow permeating throughout. I felt waves of laughter and fun echoing to my bones.

The final room was money, which began as gold coins that were hard and stuck together. They then disappeared, and in their place, paper money appeared, which also then disappeared, and finally, I saw digital money moving around in swirls. It wanted to come inside of me, up through my root chakra, moving up my body before coming out of my heart, spreading out to the world, then going back inside of my base and back around. It felt unlimited, limitless – abundant and overflowing. I then noticed the room was rainbow colours and could shift based on what I was feeling.

I felt so held and supported, and all I had to do to create a reality

I desire was to feel the feelings of what I wanted – deeply, right to my core.

EMBODIED WEALTH RESOURCE

If you would like to experience the cave of abundance for yourself, I have a guided visualisation which you can find on my Insight Timer channel. Details are in the resources section at the end.

The gentle disruptor

Take a breath and gently close your eyes, then begin to feel yourself slowly entering your heart.

Find yourself in this powerful cocoon, this space of possibility, this portal to the Divine.

From here, roots go down deep into the earth – connecting your heart with the heart of our Great Mother.

A cord connects you to the Cosmos – its milky starriness a blueprint for your creations, embedded within.

You are held. Connected. Supported.

Lie back into the deep waters of your heart. A space that feels like the bottom of the ocean. A place of peace and stillness.

You don't need to push or force anymore.
You don't need to try to make things happen.
Let all that you have been carrying, holding together for so long, so strongly – go.
Let it be taken by the waters.

Breathe.
Be you.
Just you.
Perfectly you.

The power of things

We collect, accumulate, acquire possessions. Things. Stuff. Belongings. Items that invoke memories, that make us feel something, that give us a sense of safety and security.

I recently got rid of all of my childhood and teen items – and in hindsight, felt I had been a little ruthless – but it made me realise how much power we give to our belongings. How much they mean to us as they have this ability to bring up so much.

I started to wonder if, in ancient times (Atlantis, to be precise), we were able to put our power into objects. Was this why we have such an attachment to belongings? I certainly feel the energy of items, and how something can change a room, or bring up a feeling or an emotion.

A lot of advertising certainly plays on this need to create a feeling by acquiring more, more, more. I totally get the need and want to have items that mean a lot to us, but I also ask you to consider where you might be giving your power away to things.

Water power

There's so much power in water.
It soothes.
It holds.
It heals.

It flushes.
It cleanses.
It washes away.

Creation comes from the water.
It is the cocoon that holds us before being born.
It carries the energy of emotions.
It carries the energy of intention.

There's so much power available to us in water if we choose.

BLUE

I choose...

To know I am always deeply supported.
To let go of beliefs that I have taken on or that no longer resonate.
To release stories that keep me small and limited.
To notice and be grateful for the abundance everywhere.
To do what it takes to come back to myself always.
To step into the truth of who I am.
To embody my unique essence fully.
To live a life of limitless potential.
To embody my magnetic Goddess energy.
To embody my creative power.
To know it's always working out for me.
To receive my deepest desires.
To let it be easy.
To let it be fun and joyful.
To always just be ME.

What do you choose?

It is time to speak up

For all those who came before who couldn't speak up.
It is time to speak for them.

For all those who don't have a voice.
It is time to speak for them.

For all those who were burned or persecuted for speaking their truth.
It is time to speak for them.

For all those who, to this day, aren't listened to or heard.
It is time to speak for them.

For yourself – your truth, what you stand for.
It is time to speak for you.

Your voice carries power.
Your voice carries wisdom.
Let your voice be heard.
It is time to speak up.

Voicing your needs

As I move closer to my moon time, I feel a cauldron of emotions – anger, rage, fury, deep sadness, waves of grief. The feminine yin parts which need peace, softness, solitude, and rest are still so denied, ignored, and brushed aside.

They are a part of my wholeness.
They are a part of the cyclical nature of this planet.
They are a part of all of us.

I let the anger come up to be released.
To be let go.
I need to fucking scream, scream, scream.
I cry, I release, for all the times I had no voice, where I wasn't heard or listened to, not respected for feeling this way. For all the others who had to ignore their needs, who still have to ignore their needs and push through, doing it in a way that goes against all their natural instincts.

No longer.
I choose to speak up.
I choose to declare my needs.
I choose to honour my rhythmic nature.

Every time you express and voice your needs, honouring your true nature, you heal the wounds of separation from our cyclical blueprint and pave the way for a more harmonious relationship with Earth and each other.

NDIGO

Four seasons of the moon

The minute I entered the mysterious deep blue waters glistening under a silvery moon, I felt like my legs were being burnt. A prickling sensation quickly travelled up to my lower back and then around to my belly. I felt like I was being burned alive for being me. The heat began to centre around my womb-space, and felt like I was a midwife or a doula, a keeper of creation, and it was not safe to be that. I was being burned alive. I then instantly heard the words, 'Let that go.'

It released, and I was taken to another scene, a Mystery School, where I had magical powers. One of the teachers knew about the powers and wanted to use me for them. I didn't want this, I wanted them for the Earth, for the animals, to help others. But there was fear and blackmail, and in the end, I had to hide them, say they were gone, so they couldn't be abused. Then something rose around feeling like a fraud, and others thinking they are being swindled if I share my gifts and my power. Again I heard the words, 'Let that go.'

Letting it dissolve into the waters, the next scene I was taken to was on the Titanic, where I was with the love of my life. He drowned when the ship sank, and I lost him forever. A belief was created that bad things happened when you find love. Again the words echoed, 'Let that go,' along with, 'Bad things do NOT happen when you find love.'

In the last vision I was taken to, I was a kid playing at home. My father had died at war, and my mother was doing herself up to try and find a new husband. The only way to find a husband was to look as pretty as you could. She ended up with a new man who abused and hurt her greatly. The belief was created that it's not safe to be pretty and beautiful. The words 'let that go' quickly came up again.

As I let those experiences dissolve into the water, I then was guided to submerge my head and let the waters hold me fully. I felt the earth beneath me, the moon above, and the tides of the ocean lapping around me. When it was time to come up, I felt the power and the knowing that it's time to own all of me.

Be you

You came here for a reason.
You came here to make a difference.
You came here for change.
You came here to be you.

Stop dimming your light.
Stop getting stuck in all the stories.
Stop playing small.
Stop letting others define you.

See yourself back in the womb.
Hear your heartbeat attuning to Mother Earth's.
That lifeforce, energy and support are always there to guide you.
Now feel yourself being re-born into the you that you came here to be.

Own it.
Embody it.
Be it.
Believe it.

Just, be you.

Galactic heritage

The water was a glowing turquoise with sparkles shimmering on the surface. There was no separation between the waters and the galaxies, and I felt myself going upwards, further into the deep cosmic watery-ness.

I suddenly became very aware that I was surrounded by my star family, in particular my cosmic mother. I felt her powerful but gentle presence. She said she has always been here with me. She said she's so proud of the journey I have been on. The courage and growth I have experienced. She told me that she is holding me always – all of my cosmic family are, and I just need to reach out if ever I need reminding.

They have my back, they are to support me as I step into my power. As I take action. As I speak up. As I follow my guidance and do what I am being called to.

Your cosmic family is also here for you. Reach out to them, feel them. Lean on your galactic heritage to support you.

Make a wish

When you were a child, did you believe in magic?
Did you see magic everywhere? From the stars to bubbles in the bathtub?
Did you feel you were magical?
Did you know you were magical?

Let me remind you that you are.

You are a powerful manifestor and can speak your wishes into existence.
The power of your voice connected to your heart's desire is potent fuel for your magical self.

Tune into the rhythm of your heart.
Ask it what it wants.
Let it communicate with you in its own unique way.
Then speak your wish out loud.

Now let yourself receive it. Take the action you are guided to as a co-creator. Let it come about.

But most of all, accept your power as a creator.
Accept that you are magical.
Accept that you are worthy of it.
Accept your whole self.

VIOLET

Grief becomes you

Sometimes life hits you with experiences that can feel like explosions in your heart.
They leave you questioning it all – 'Why and how can this have happened?'
Life as you knew it has now taken a different trajectory.
Life as you knew it will never be the same again.

Then the grief comes in.
It can be all-consuming.
Take over, and become you.
You might begin to feel defined by it.
It will certainly shape you.

You start to mirror the experience in different ways, shapes, and forms.
Perhaps you start to believe you are un-deserving of any good.
Maybe you become cynical, over-controlling, and un-trusting.
You begin to embody a version of you who isn't their fullest.
You begin to embody a version who has dulled and numbed their sparkle.

When grief becomes you.
It's almost impossible to remember your truth.
It's almost impossible to remember your greatness.
It's almost impossible to have hope.
It's almost impossible to find the light.

Let yourself be carried by it.
Let it move and be expressed through you.
Acknowledge it. Feel it. Release it.
Voice it. Wail it. Scream it.

Then surrender to its holding-like cocoon, to metamorphosise, to transform, to be re-born.

When the time is right, you will emerge.
More powerful than ever.

What did you come here to experience?

I invite you to tune into the time before time, the space before you arrived in this body, the essence of your being as it chose to be born.

What experiences did you come here to have?

I invite you to tune into the desires of your heart, the feelings you wish to have, the emotions you want to feel.

What experiences did you come here to have?

Where are you not allowing yourself to experience these things? The richness and wealth you desire in all areas of your life – health, home, relationships, money, creativity, all the things. Where are you holding back from allowing yourself to receive and experience it? Or perhaps judging and assuming it's not possible, or not possible for you?

You can always find what you wish to experience within your body, and allow it to show you where you might have resistance, as well as what it does feel like, to bring it closer.

EMBODIED WEALTH PRACTICE

Spend a moment connecting to one thing you would like to experience more of in your life. Notice how it feels and where you feel it in your body. Acknowledge it and allow it to get bigger.

Do you notice any resistance? Any thoughts rising, telling you that you can't have it? Are you willing to let these feelings go? Are you willing to re-write this story/pattern/belief? Set the intention to do that, which may involve action on your part, as well as guidance in some way.

Now connect to the feeling of the experience deeply in your body. Hold it, be with it, feel it, embody it for as long as feels good. Then when you are ready you can ask 'Is there any aligned action I can take to bring this closer?' Trust the guidance you receive (and if there is none, that is fine too), then do what you are guided to.

For example, you may want to experience more freedom in your life. This might start with a feeling of your heart and chest opening. As you breathe into it you might start to feel expansive, limitless, as though you are carefree and open to all possibilities.

As your body feels this, thoughts might pop up like, 'Who are you to have this? You have a job and responsibilities, and you don't earn enough money to ever feel like this. You don't know enough. The world doesn't work in this way,' etc., etc., etc.

Be willing to see a new way, to let this go, to align with a new possibility. It may require some belief work (which you can see more on in the introduction section). It will require you to believe in a new way. Guidance might come in from different places – for example, you might read, hear, or see something that inspires you to try something new.

Then keep connecting to that feeling of freedom. Let your body feel it, breathe it, expand it, embody it. The guidance you receive to bring it into your life will vary. Some examples are: being guided to let something go, to start something new, to keep trusting, to keep connecting. Let yourself be led exactly where you are.

The prostitute

There was a woman shackled, metal chains around her bony ankles, her soles were dirty, there were stains on her pasty skin, and rags falling off her limbs. She lay on a bare mattress, so worn the springs were sticking out in places.

She was there, a prisoner of the church, for disobeying their rules.

She had been a prostitute and then run a brothel. She had enjoyed the good life of drinking, partying, and indulging in every way. She had been a larger-than-life character who lived for pleasure, sheer and utter orgasmic pleasure, and joy.

Something had happened to her, and she now carried so much shame. She carried the burden of guilt. Of having lived a life of excess and more than others. She felt she now deserved this punishment. To be separate, living in exile. To be living the extreme opposite of her former life. She now needed to repent for her sins.

As this woman lay there, I could feel her shame and guilt permeating the air. It cast a thick gloomy spell in the surrounding area, beyond the walls of her confines. It was an amplifying energy that stopped any plants nearby from being able to grow. Nature didn't want to – nor could it – grow in that stench.

Then a voice came in and said, 'Receiving pleasure, joy, and abundance is the catalyst for you to bring more of it into the world. By allowing yourself to receive what you desire, you create a ripple effect and give others permission to have it too. You shift the energy around you.'

The energy began to change, the woman softened and started to return to her former self. Desire began to flow through her veins, a beat of pleasure vibrated from her heart, and colour returned to her skin.

She broke free of the constricts, leaping out of the cell back into the world, which, mirroring her, began bursting with life and abundance as she deeply felt the truth in those words.

MAGENTA

Being present in the body

Little bubbles of love and support surrounded me. I felt held by them.

Then I suddenly felt very aware of my body, and this deep, deep appreciation and love for all parts of it. As I sat with that feeling, it turned into pockets of pleasure. Little vortexes of sensuality swirling throughout, right to my core.

This presence, stillness, and awareness of myself inside my body was so simple yet felt utterly profound.

I reflected on my journey with Covid, and then long Covid, in which I had to care for my body on a whole new level. I had to put it first daily; nurturing it through nourishment and movement; letting it lead and guide me; being kind, gentle and compassionate with it. This was it. This was all my body ever wanted, and since showing it this love and care, it became a home I truly felt comfortable in for the first time ever.

I felt a stillness, a being-ness, and deep contentment in simply being alive in a body. I felt so held by my body – it felt like a moment of ecstasy coupled with a blanket of warmth and calm.

Smell the roses

All the over-doing makes me so fucking angry.
The constant need to give, to prove, to assert, to compete, to do, do, do.
It's all so exhausting.
It's damn-right depleting.

What if we all just stopped for a moment.
Stopped filling the spaces.
Stopped do-ing, just to do.
Slowed the fuck down.
Stopped and smelled those metaphorical (and real) roses.

It doesn't all need to happen right now.
It doesn't all need to happen this week.

Take a breath. Take a pause.

It's time to be.
It's time to tune in.
It's time to connect to your truth.

What is that for you right now?

To be or to do, that is the question

Be.
Do.
Be.
Do.
Be.
Do.
Be.
Do.
Be.
Do.
Be.
Do.
Be.
Do.
Be.
Do.
Be.
Do.
Be.
Do.

EMBODIED WEALTH PROMPT

What are you truly being guided towards in this moment?

Love, wisdom, and power

You are love.
You are wisdom.
You are power.

You carry it in your flesh, your bones, your cells, your energy.

Let yourself remember this.
Let it activate deep within.
Let yourself become it.
Let yourself embody it.

Then watch as the world begins to remind you of this truth.

Who did you come here to be?

There's a part of you that knows.
There's a part of you that feels it.
There's a part of you that has no doubts whatsoever about who you
came here to be.

It's what comes naturally to you.
It makes you sparkle on the outside and glow on the inside.
It lights a fire in your whole damn being.

You could talk about it endlessly.
Scream about it from the rooftops.
You want to help others with it.

Or perhaps you just know it.
It just is.
It is you.

So often, we equate our careers or roles in society with who we
are. But there's something, or maybe more than one thing, inside
of you that is a part of who you came here to be. You might know
it from when you were a child. Perhaps it's a memory from a one-
time experience. It might be something you have yet to discover.
It might also be simply, but powerfully, about your presence, your
energy, your way of being.

I invite you to own it and embody it, as I see it as a part of the wealth
of who you came here to be.

LILAC

Creating through the senses

I felt myself connected to the Earth, and a spiral came down from my root chakra at the base of my body, grounding me deep within. The spiral then began to move upwards, swirling and reaching far out into the Cosmos. I felt the power of creation within every inch of my body, as above and below.

From this place of connection, I was shown how we create within our bodies, through our senses: smells, tastes, feelings, sounds, visions – no matter which one/s you connect with the most. The experience created by our senses is how we create.

So by vividly imagining and feeling as many of your senses turned on with what you wish to bring into your life (creating a multi-sensory experience), you begin to create it – first within, and then in time, it will come to be mirrored on the outside.

You are safe

There might be memories of turbulence, tossing and turning.
Your body might remember all the times you were not safe.
There may have been times when you weren't safe to be you.
To speak up, to be in your body, to be here.

Honouring you deeply for all that you remember and have
experienced.

Find the safety within your body.
Acknowledge the parts that remember the fear, the uncertainty,
the not knowing.
Imagine a light of holding and comfort surrounding them.
Let them loosen their grip, release and let go.

You are safe, you are safe, you are safe.

You were born to fly

Sometimes it can feel so scary to truly take that leap and fly. Let everything go that's weighing you down. Let yourself 'be' all that you know you are inside.

You might fear that you will fall and nobody will catch you.
You might fear that you'll be all alone when you begin to fly.
You might think you are afraid of heights, and not meant to soar.
You might feel dizzy and nauseous as you begin to expand.

But dear one, you were born to fly.
So spread these wings, take that leap, and let yourself fly.

Stepping into what's possible

Who is the most expansive, limitless, free-est version of you?

How do they describe themselves?

What do they do that you don't do?

What don't they do that you still do?

How do they treat themself?

How do they look after themself?

How do they show up daily?

What would it take for you to begin to embody this version of you right now?

WHITE

Bubble stories

Imagine your body is filled with bubbles. Bubbles each containing the different stories, beliefs, patterns, thoughts, and behaviours that you have picked up from others. The things that have been a part of your conditioning. Stories telling you that you don't deserve to be happy; beliefs affirming that you aren't worthy of love; things making you feel, who are you to have it all. You are filled from top to toe with all of these bubbles. Some are bigger than others. Some are denser and fuller.

Thank these bubbles for all they are carrying. They have held you and kept you safe for one reason or another.
But now it's time to release them. Let them go. You don't need them anymore.

Begin by inviting liquid diamond white light to fill you up from above. As it does, there is no space for the bubbles as well, and they begin to dissipate – being pushed out or simply popping into the ethers.

Now, connect to this truth, to this space in between. The stories are gone, and there is emptiness left. Take a moment to breathe in this being-ness.

Feel the shift. Feel the peace. Feel the stillness.

This is you.

Love is all around

You are the soft, gentle innocence of a baby.
You are a child of the Divine.
You are so supported and held by your ancestors.
You are so deeply loved.
If only you knew the love that surrounds you at all times, you wouldn't question your worthiness for even a second.

Take a moment and breathe in this support and love, beloved one.

Levelling up

Who is the version of you that feels safe, held and grounded?
Who is the version of you who has fierce boundaries?
Who is the version of you that is connected to their creative and sexual energy?
Who is the version of you that owns their power?
Who is the version of you that knows their worth?
Who is the version of you that is compassionate and caring towards others, and to themselves?
Who is the version of you that speaks their truth?
Who is the version of you that trusts their path deeply, knowing they are so supported?
Who is the version of you that knows who the fuck they are?

The wealth in between

There's wealth in the just be-ing, the pockets in between.
There's unlimited possibility in that liminal space before the momentum occurs.
It's like a ball of energy ready to be channelled.
It's pure creative potential, that can be shaped in whatever way you choose.

It's a moment to also be savoured and felt.
Allowed to be there without trying to change it, force it, or do anything.
There's beauty in the stillness, the noise-less, the void.
Let it wash over you, spreading into each and every one of your cells.

Nowhere to go. Nothing to do.
Simply be with it. Breathe it in.
Honour its presence.
When it is ready, you will know.

Let it be the blank canvas for your desires.
You can mould it in any way you choose.
Give to it feelings, emotions, colours, visuals, sounds and more.
Harnessing your power as a co-creator.
Claiming your I AM.

FINAL THOUGHTS

Thank you, dear reader, for getting here, or maybe you just opened the book up on this page. Either way, I am so honoured that these words found their way to you.

I hope that you have been inspired by this way of looking at and feeling into what wealth is.
True wealth, in my opinion.

I hope that you see the possibility for us all to create a wealthy life, which starts from within. Yes, it might be easier, simpler even, for some to do this than others, but as we begin with ourselves, taking that first step, which then adds up, leading to significant change, we show others what's possible, and we can truly start to create a ripple effect of worldwide wealth. That's my vision anyway.

Above all, I hope it reminds you that you are more powerful than you might ever have been led to believe. You can create a wealthy life. You can feel and experience all the things you desire to. Let the wisdom of your body, mind, soul, and heart guide you, and remember, you are a powerful creator.

Remember your I AM...

FURTHER RESOURCES AND WAYS TO CONNECT WITH ME

My books – All available anywhere you buy your books online

Embodied – A self-care guide for sensitive souls
Embodied Business – A guide to grounding and aligning your business chakras for empathpreneurs
Embodied Creation – The sensitive's way to consciously co-create

My oracle card deck – Available at bit.ly/embodied-wisdom

Embodied Wisdom - A colour alchemy card deck to bring you into alignment with your truth

Insight Timer – My meditations are available here: https://insighttimer.com/loveembodied.

Colour Mirrors – www.colourmirrors.com

You can also get in touch with me if you would like one-to-one or group support (I offer a number of programmes, courses and workshops). You can find me at www.empathpreneurs.org. There you will find links to all my socials, so you can choose your preferred one if I am on it (Instagram is currently my favourite, but that might change).

There is also a resources page with a number of offers and freebies that might inspire and support you.

AUTHOR BIO - TARA JACKSON

I am someone who cares deeply about all living beings and this planet. I sometimes despair at the state of the world, as I feel so much and want to help everyone. I need lots of reminders to come back to the present moment. Journaling, forest-bathing, being in and around water in all forms, and movement are my current go-to practices to support me with this.

I love to create and am happiest when I am tuned into the energies of the Cosmos and Earth, as muses for my creations, whatever form they might take. You might have also guessed I LOVE colour and like to infuse it into every area of my life. I need lots (and it seems to be increasing) of time alone to ground, rest and replenish, but also couldn't live without my deep, soulful one-to-one connections with people who also get to the shit that matters fast and don't do small talk!

On the professional side, I am an intuitive business mentor, holistic wellbeing coach, artist, and author who supports empathpreneurs with releasing, healing, and letting go of all that is stopping them from fully claiming their magic and co-creating the business (and life) of their dreams, that considers all and our home. (Oh yes, that is a mouthful as I speak and think quite fast, and consciously have to slow down)!

ACKNOWLEDGEMENTS

There are so many incredible humans that have contributed to, moved, inspired, triggered (thank you, especially, to the ones who have triggered), and supported me on my ongoing journey, and I know there will be more. To each and every one of you, thank you! You have brought me closer to coming home to myself.

I want to thank a few people in particular who have been there for me as I brought this book into the world, in the incredibly short space that it made itself known and wanted to be birthed.

Meron, thank you for being the first person I reluctantly shared *Embodied Wealth* with, as I was still catching my breath after the birthing of *Embodied Creation*. Thank you for seeing and saying that you also felt it wanted to come so soon. Thank you for the space you have held for me to share throughout, and it still blows me away how I was staying with you as the words finally began to flow. You have truly been the midwife for this baby!

Oh Nicola, it's been quite the ride with this Embodied series, huh!? Thank you for the alchemical space you have held for me, for leading this way and for being such a big part of my journey. I am so honoured to have you as the Godmother of my Embodied babies. This has to be the last one, right?! ;-)

Lele, you are the best. Thank you for everything always and for putting up with my super-sensitivity, my tantrums when I didn't want to write, and for letting me use your bedroom and space to pull this final book together. You are too kind to me, I love you!

Dad, I am so grateful for you. You get the way I am, the way I work and how I have to honour the energy of my creations. I love that I get to share them with you, and thank you for always championing me and being the first person to read everything I write.

Katherine, thank you for being in my life, for being my 'twin' and for supporting me always. Your wisdom, insights, space-holding and guidance have enabled me to bring this book into what it needed and wanted to be.

Lynda, you always nail the vision for the cover – I am so thankful to you, for all of my beautiful, colourful covers! Jesse, thank you so much again for editing these words and helping me to bring it even closer to birthing.

To the rest of the incredible The Unbound Press team, who I know will be weaving their magic into the journey of *Embodied Wealth* as it makes its way into the world, Sarah, Jo and Em in particular, I thank you all in advance.

Thank you to my family for all being so supportive of all my writing endeavours. I am grateful for you all.

Lastly, the hugest thank you to the wonderful early reviewers, I am truly honoured to include your feedback and energy in these pages.

Lightning Source UK Ltd.
Milton Keynes UK
UKHW021839090922
408609UK00004B/8

9 781913 590659